DESIGN
D&T
MAKE IT!

product design
for key stage 3

ANDY BIGGS

MELANIE FASCIATO

TRISTRAM SHEPARD

First published in 2000 by:
Nelson Thornes Ltd
Delta Place
27 Bath Road
Cheltenham
GL53 7TH

04 / 5 4 3

A catalogue record of this book is available from the British Library.

ISBN 0 7487 4429 0

Designed and typeset by Carla Turchini
Picture research by John Bailey
Artwork by Tristram Ariss, Hardlines, Mike Gordon, John Fowler and Anna Roberts
Printed and bound in China by Midas Printing International Ltd.

The authors would like to thank the following people: Staff and pupils at Cheadle Hulme College and Cheadle and Presdales School, Ware, Herts.

Where specific retailer's and manufacturer's products have been used to illustrate industrial practice they are not intended to imply any endorsement.

The publishers are grateful to the following for permission to reproduce photographs and other copyright material: Action Plus p.98 (bottom left); Alison Page pp.140 (bottom right), 141 (top left, top right, bottom right); Allsport p.46 (bottom left); Aquarius Photolibrary p.46 (middle right); Apple pp.69, 140 (top left); Automobile Association p.83; Architectural Association p.102 (bottom – Carol Shields); British Gas p.83; British Steel p.102 (middle); Bay Gen pp.136, 137; Berghaus p.138 (bottom left); Cannon Shelley p.54 (top); Dyson pp.114, 115 (for further information contact Dyson Press Office, 20 Shawfield Street, London SW3 4DB); Disabled Living Foundation p.116; ECM Records p.68 (bottom – Michael Manoogian); Economics (Education) Ltd pp. 133, 140 (top right); Focal Design Studios pp. 92, 93; Fisher p.134 (left); Ford p.83; Goliath Games p.47; Guido Cecere p.54 (bottom); Hutchison Photolibrary p.30 (middle); Help the Aged p.116; Levi's p.83; LEGO pp.64, 65; Martyn Chillmaid pp.18 (bottom right), 19 (middle), 20 (middle), 26, 38, 40 (top and bottom), 42, 43, 50 (bottom right), 51 (top right), 55, 57, 62, 63 (top), 78, 91, 93, 95, 100 (top right and left), 104 (top left and right), 105 (top and bottom right), 112, 113 (right), 119 (top right and bottom), 122, 126 (bottom left), 128, 132, 134 (right), 139 (bottom right); Mars p.6 (top left); Microsoft Corporation p.140 (bottom right); NEFF p.118; Network Photographers pp. 44 (Georg Gerster), 45 (bottom – Georg Gerster); Oxfam p.116; Panasonic p.119 (top); Panos Pictures p.51 (bottom left – Jean-Leo Dugast); Photographers Library p.30 (top); RSPCA p.116; Robert Harding Picture Library pp.28 (bottom centre – Tim Hall), 103 (bottom left – Roy Rainford), 121 (top – Tony Demin, International Stock); Retna p.46 (middle centre – Craig Barritt); Rochdale Libraries p.96 (top left and bottom left); Rover Group p.96 (bottom right); Science Museum p.96 (top right); Science Photolibrary pp.16 (top right – Robert Hernadez), 61 (bottom – Alfred Pasieka), 111 (Maximilian Stock Ltd), 131 (Bruce Iverson), 140 (bottom left – Maximilian Stock Ltd); Sony Music Entertainment p.68 (top – Dave Gibbons); Sporting Pictures p.46 (top left – R Widner); Stockmarket pp.28 (top right, top left, bottom left), 61 (top), 109 (T Horowitz); Swizzels Matlow pp.92, 93; Stanley Tools pp.19 (bottom), 22 (top); Stone pp.45 (top – Thomas J Peterson), 51 (top left – David Woodfall), 97 (middle right – Michael Rosenfeld); Telegraph Colour Library pp.7 (bottom right – Benelux Press, 28 (bottom right), 31 (bottom – S Benbow), 51 (bottom right – Benelux Press), 108 (L Lefkowitz), 123 (L Lefkowitz); Topham Picturepoint pp.34, 107 (right); Tetra Pak p.16 (bottom); The Body Shop p.83; TRIP pp. 30 (bottom – H Rogers), 31 (top – H Rogers), 100 (bottom – J Wender), 101 (H Rogers), 104 (middle right – M Azavedo) (bottom – M Peters), 106 (H Rogers), 107 (left – H Rogers), 121 (bottom – K Jones); Umbro International p.46 (bottom); WHSmith p.83; Volkswagen p.97 (top right).

Every effort has been made to contact copyright holders. The publishers apologise to anyone whose rights have been overlooked and will be happy to rectify any errors or omissions at the earliest opportunity.

Contents

Introduction

Welcome to **Design & Make It! Product Design for Key Stage 3**. This book will help you succeed in Design and Technology. It tells you all you need to know about working with resistant materials, electronics and graphics when designing and making products.

How to use this book

The book starts by explaining about Product Design. The **Project Guide** which follows will be useful throughout your course. It explains the different design and making aspects of a Product Design project. You will be assessed on these skills.

The book is then divided into six **units**. Each unit begins by setting you a design challenge. What you will need to do to meet the challenge is explained. The pages which follow will:

▷ tell you what you need to know
▷ set tasks for you to do
▷ remind you how to keep a record of what you do.

Each unit focuses on a different area of Product Design:

Unit 1 is concerned with working with wood, and involves designing and making a message pad holder.

The focus in **Unit 2** is structures, electronics and systems. You will be designing and making a decorative object for a celebration.

Unit 3 involves using wood and plastic to design and make a pocket-sized maze game.

Unit 4 is about graphics and structures. Here you will be designing and making a menu and other items for a chain of new high street cafés.

The focus in **Unit 5** is batch production. Can you design and make a flower holder in quantity?

Unit 6 is about mechanisms and electronics. It involves designing and making a moving money box for charity.

The final section is the **Product Design Dictionary**. It explains and illustrates the special words and phrases often used in Product Design. Words printed in **red type** in the book are included in this dictionary.

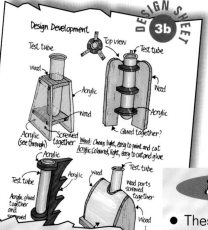

Examples of pupils' work from design sheets are often provided. These will give you a good idea of the sort of work you need to do.

● On task

These sections will set you tasks to do. Sometimes they will be practical. Sometimes they will ask you to find out more about existing products. Your teacher will tell you which tasks you need to do and when.

On your design sheets

- These boxes will remind you what you need to put on paper as part of your design folder.

- You will be encouraged to use coloured sketches, charts and diagrams as well as words.

- Where more than one design sheet is used, this is shown as: **3b**.

Remember

- These boxes will help you revise what you have learned.

- They provide a summary of the key points you need to know.

What is Product Design?

Product Design is one area within the subject called Design and Technology. All areas of Design and Technology involve designing and making things.

We are surrounded by products. The clothes we wear, the food we eat, the tables and chairs we sit at are all things that someone has designed, and that have been made for us.

This book is about designing certain types of products:

▷ 3D products

▷ electronic products and systems

▷ graphic products.

3D products

These products are made from what are sometimes called 'resistant' materials, such as wood, metals and plastics. Ceramics and glass are also resistant materials, though not covered here.

There are many familiar examples of these sorts of products, for example, furniture, jewellery, containers, toys and games, and household utensils. Larger items such as cars could also come under this heading.

To design and make these sorts of products it's important to know about the working properties and characteristics of a range of materials, so you can choose which will be best to use. You also need to become familiar with the tools and manufacturing processes used to prepare, cut, shape, form and assemble them.

Electronic products and systems

These products are similar to 3D products, except they involve the use of electronic components as well. Electronic systems can sense things like sound, movement and light, and switch circuits on and off.

Computer games, mobile telephones, personal stereos and TV remote controls are all examples of familiar electronic products.

Designing electronic products involves:

▷ choosing the right components to put together to make something happen

▷ making a suitable container for them, to keep them safe, and make them easy to use.

How much do you know already about mechanical systems?

Graphic products

Graphic products are things like books, magazines, calendars, menus, sales brochures and packaging. They tend to be two-dimensional, and are made from paper or card that has been printed on. Sometimes the flat surface is cut and folded and made up into a three-dimensional shape (e.g. a 'pop-up' card, or a box).

Designing graphic products involves:

▷ choosing colours and textures and different styles and sizes of lettering

▷ arranging words and illustrations together on a page

▷ knowing about the properties and characteristics of different graphic media and materials (e.g. pens, paints, chalks, papers and cards).

Information and communication technology (ICT)

Designers use computers and other related devices a great deal. They help speed up the process of designing and making something. They also make accuracy easier to achieve. You should try to use computers in your design projects.

It's not always appropriate to use a computer, however. Sometimes it's better to sketch on paper, or to experiment with some real materials or electronic components.

Manufacturing

Through the book you will be introduced to the idea of manufacturing. It's one thing to make a single product in your school workshop but quite another to work out how 100, 1,000 or 100,000 might be made in a factory.

Working together

Products are rarely designed and made by just one person. It usually involves different teams of people, all working together. As you do the projects in the book you will often be invited to share ideas, discuss problems, and take on different roles in making something. You will learn more about how to communicate and co-operate to get a job done on time.

Product analysis

Designers learn a great deal from studying products that have already been designed and made. They work out what is successful, and what hasn't worked. They then try to make their own designs better.

Try to get into the habit of looking at some of the many products that surround you, and asking how well they have been designed and made.

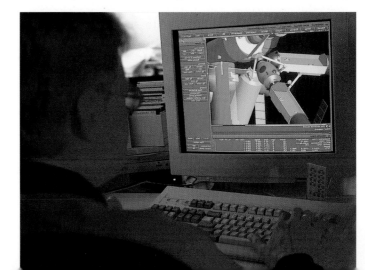

Project Guide

◎ Investigate

In your D&T projects you will need to do some investigation to learn more about:
• the consumers you are designing for
• what they need and want
• what the product might be made from and how it might be made.

To do this you will have to:
• observe and talk to your target consumer group
• consult books, leaflets, booklets, etc.
• contact experts for advice
• use CD-ROMs, software and the Internet.

As you plan and carry out investigation work you need to keep asking yourself whether you are finding out the **right** information. It must be **relevant** to your project.

To investigate something means to examine, inquire or find out more about it.

As you design and develop your ideas, make sure you take into account the things you have discovered in your investigation.

◎ Have good ideas

Having good ideas of your own is a very important part of work in Design and Technology.
Experiment with different materials and methods. Think of lots of possible ideas – don't just choose your first idea.

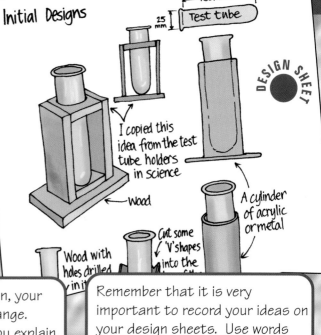

Initial Designs

150mm

25 mm   Test tube

I copied this idea from the test tube holders in science

Wood

A cylinder of acrylic or metal

DESIGN SHEET

Cut some 'V'shapes into the...

Wood with holes drilled in it

You also need to think about the **design specification** and the **conflicting demands** within it. Look in the dictionary on page 138 and 139 for more information about these.

As you design, your ideas will change. Make sure you explain why you decided to change them.

Remember that it is very important to record your ideas on your design sheets. Use words and sketches together. Use colour to help explain your ideas.

Develop your design

As you start to finalise your design ideas you need to **test them out**. It would be crazy to make a batch of 100 new mechanical toys if you hadn't tried the mechanism out first.

If possible, people from your target consumer group should test your product and say what they think about it.

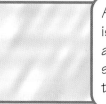

As always, **presenting your ideas** is very important. You need to be able to show your notes and sketches to other people to get their comments and suggestions.

Exactly what do you want to learn from your tests? What do you need to do to get the information you want?

Your work needs to be clear and concise. It needs to show the features of your design: who it's for, its components and how it would be made.

Apply what you know (designing)

So what **do** you know already about working with resistant and graphic materials, and electronics? Probably a lot more than you think.

As you work through your projects you will learn a lot about the **properties and characteristics** of the different materials and processes you use. You will get to know what works best and why.

On your design sheets you need to make it clear how you are applying what you know to your work.

Evaluate

Evaluating products that already exist will help you understand **how** and **why** they have been designed that way.

It's a good idea to **compare** an existing product to other similar products. You should also say what other people say about it. Their views might be different from yours. Include the results of testing.

You will be able to use what you have discovered to help you come up with ideas for a new product.

When you evaluate an existing product you need to do more than just describe it. Make sure you also comment on its **quality** – how successful it is. Try to use as many descriptive words as possible.

You also need to evaluate **your own ideas** as you develop your designs. On your design sheet you need to record things such as:
- which your best ideas are, and why
- how well your ideas might work
- what you plan to do next as a result of evaluating your own work.

Project Guide

◎ Plan the making

Planning what you are doing is a very important aspect of Design and Technology project work. There are so many things to do you have to work out what **order** to do them in, and **how long** to spend doing them.

Where might **difficulties** occur? What would you do if you ran out of a particular material? At what stages could you check the **quality** of what you were making? Where will you include safety checks?

Make a list of all the things you need to do. Try to sort the list into **main stages** of production – preparing the materials and joining them, etc. Then put the things you need to do in order within each main stage.

Planning the Making

DESIGN SHEET

① Use the template to mark out the design onto acrylic

② Use the template to mark out th design onto M.D.F.

③

④

What needs doing first? What can be done later? How much time do you need to allow for drying, etc.

Record your planning work on your design sheets. You may need to change your plans when things don't go as expected. Be sure to explain what you did and why.

◎ Apply what you know (making)

From previous work you have done you should know about things such as:
• the need for safety in workshops
• different production methods.

How can you use what you already know about working with resistant and graphic materials, and electronics?

This is where you need to make sure you try to choose the best materials and tools to make the product you have designed.

You need to match what you know about the characteristics and properties of materials with the tools and equipment you know you will be able to use.

Materials and Finishes

DESIGN SHEET

The base

This will be made from M.D.F. It will stay flat and it is easy to paint.

The sides

These will be made from softwood. Softwood is cheap and comes from sustainable forests. It can be varnished to show up the grain.

The cover

On your design sheets you need to make it clear how you are applying what you know to your making.

Work with materials

If you are not sure about a particular process it might be a good idea to **practise** it first before you make your final product.

As you make your products you need to **take care** while you work.

Use the tools carefully to join materials together.
Be as **accurate** as you can when you measure.
You will need to organise your tools and your workspace to make your product safely and accurately.

Pay close attention to **safety** precautions while you work.

Carefully explain how you worked on your design sheets. Say which safety precautions you took.

Final evaluation

When you tested your final product what did the people it was intended for think? Maybe they made some useful suggestions for improvements? How might you change your ideas?
Explain how you tested your final product and what happened.

At the end of your project you will need to think very carefully about how well you have done.

Finally, how well did **you** work during the project? For example:
• How thorough was your investigation?
• How different were all your ideas?
• How carefully did you plan the making?
• What were your strengths and weaknesses?

First of all consider the **product** you have designed and made.
• How **successful** is it?
• Does it solve the problem you were given at the start? If not, why not?
• Did it turn out the way you intended. If not, why not?

How could you **improve** the way you work next time? Which aspects of Design and Technology are you going to **target** in your next project? Discuss with your teacher what you will need to do to show you have made **progress**.

Starting Point

Get the Message?

A nature conservation organisation wants a new product to sell in its shops.

Can you design and make a message pad holder for them? It needs to be suitable for scrap paper and have a wildlife theme.

Here at the World Nature Organisation we believe that people should be encouraged to look after our planet. We want to sell a range of products that will spread this idea.

The first products will be message pad holders for scrap paper. This will encourage people to recycle paper.

The challenge

The World Nature Organisation has set you a challenge. Can you design and make an attractive message pad holder for scrap paper?

To meet this challenge you must think carefully about two things:

▶ how your message pad holder will hold scrap paper

▶ how you are going to make it an attractive product.

The focus

In this unit you will focus on:

▶ developing your designing and making skills using timber. You will find out how to shape materials and join them together.

▶ developing your drawing skills in two ways. You will need to draw ideas freehand, and do drawings that are neat and precise.

The end product

You will design and make a message pad holder. To be successful it must:

▶ hold at least 20 pieces of A6 scrap paper securely and attractively

▶ have an easily recognisable wildlife theme

▶ lie flat, and be able to be hung up.

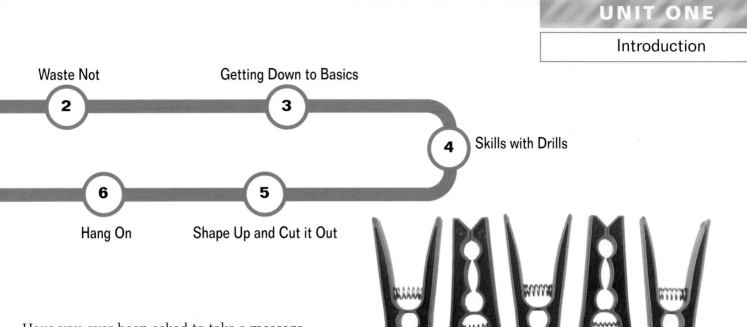

Waste Not — 2

Getting Down to Basics — 3

Skills with Drills — 4

Hang On — 6

Shape Up and Cut it Out — 5

Have you ever been asked to take a message for someone and been unable to find a piece of paper to write on?

Things To Do!
- Bank
- Library
- Dry Cleaners
- Video Shop

+ 22·
+ 30·07
+ 25·55 —
+ 75·09 — car
monthly
185·47

Sho...
• Chee...
• Hone...
• Beans
• Flo...

Bread
• Eggs
Coffee

• Juice
• Milk
• Peas

Don't Forget
Football Practice Tuesday Night
WASH KIT!!!

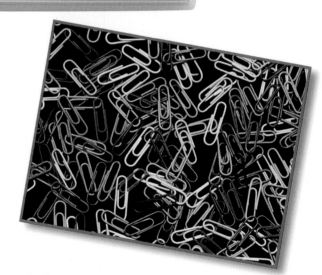

● On task Investigate

How many different ways can you think of to hold pieces of paper together?

Without using a ruler, sketch as many different methods as you can think of on design sheet **1a**.

Add labels and arrows to explain how each method works. Add some colour too.

Hold On

Get the Message?

On this page you need to explore some different ways of holding paper together.

How are you going to decide which method works best?

Did you know that the paperclip was patented in 1900 by Johann Vaaler, a Norwegian?

The World Nature Organisation want you to consider a number of different approaches to solving the problem of holding recycled scraps of paper together. They have also said it must be *portrait*.

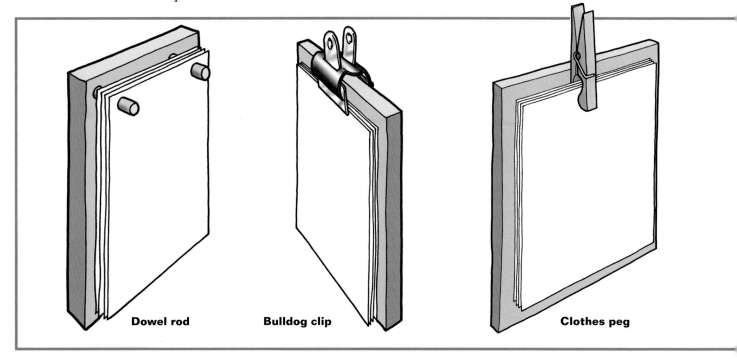

Dowel rod   Bulldog clip   Clothes peg

Which way round is which?

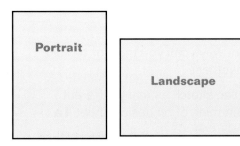

Portrait

Landscape

How large is A6 paper?
A4 paper is 210 mm by 297 mm
A5 paper is 210 mm by 148 mm
A6 paper is 105 mm by 148 mm

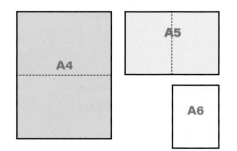

A4

A5

A6

● **On task Investigate**

Undertake the following tasks in groups of four.

1. Take turns to test each method of holding paper shown below. Fill up the chart on design sheet **1b**.

2. As a group, discuss your conclusions. At the bottom of your chart write down which method you think works best and why.

DESIGN SHEET **1b**

Criteria	Holding Method	
1 = Poor 2 = OK 3 = Excellent	Spring Peg	Bulldog Cl
Ability to grip the paper	1	3
Quantity of paper held	2	
Ease of refilling	3	
		2

Treasury tags

Can you think of any other methods of your own for solving the problem?

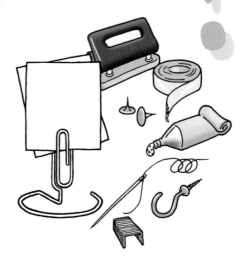

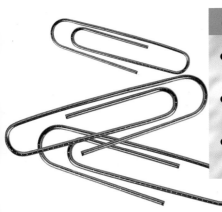

On your design sheets

- Sketch different ways of holding paper. Explain how they work. **1a**

- Write down the results of your investigation of methods of holding A6 paper. **1b**

- Say which method of holding paper you are going to use for your design. **1b**

Remember

- You need to make decisions about your design based on what you have found out in your investigations.

15

Waste Not...

Get the Message?

Before you can start to design your scrap paper message pad holder you need to discover what sort of shapes are likely to appeal to people.

Now in stock!

The World Nature Organisation have a stock of rectangular pieces of Medium Density Fibreboard (MDF), 170 mm by 220 mm. They also have a supply of dowel rods, pegs and treasury tags. They want you to use some of these items in your design.

Dispose of carefully

We need to conserve the resources we have. Recycling materials is therefore important.

Do you know what the logo on the right stands for?

Every year we simply throw unwanted products made of paper, plastic, timber, metal, etc., away. The more we recycle these materials the less damage we will do to our natural world.

Manufacturers have a responsibility to ensure that the products they make and the processes they use to make them have as little impact on the environment as possible.

Your message pad holder will help recycle scrap paper.

Tetra Pak Case Study

Tetra Pak make food packaging. As well as being safe and hygienic, their cartons are environmentally sound.

Recently they have developed a new material called Tectan. It is colourful, water-resistant and durable, and made entirely from shredded drink cartons. Tectan can be used for making many things, without having to use any new raw materials.

Getting into shape

The next stage is to develop your ideas for a suitable shape for the base-board. This shape needs to be based on a wildlife theme.

It would be easy if you were designing a message holder just for yourself. You know what your favourite animals are.

However you have to design a product that other people will want to buy. They may well have different likes and dislikes from you.

DESIGN SHEET 2b

Penguin

Teddy Bear

I like the penguin

Mum likes the bear best

Whale

Nobody liked the whale much. I think I will choose to make the penguin as it will make the best base for my paper pad.

● On task 1 Have good ideas

On design sheet **2a** draw at least three possible shapes for the base of your message pad. Base the shapes on a wildlife theme. Use books, magazines and/or a computer to find wildlife pictures. Make a note of where you found each picture.

Keep the shapes as simple as possible – remember they will need to be easy to cut out for the base-board.

● On task 2 Investigate / Evaluate

1. Show design sheet **2a** to each member of your family.

   ▶ Ask them if they can say what the animals are.

   ▶ Which one would they prefer to have as a message pad holder?

   Make a note of their comments on the sheet.

2. At the bottom of your sheet say which design you are going to choose, and why.

On your design sheets

● Draw possible shapes for the base of your message pad. **2a**

● Record the comments people made about them. **2b**

● Say which design you have chosen, and why. **2b**

Remember

● You need to find out about what people need and want before you can design things for them.

Getting Down to Basics

Get the Message?

Now you can start to make the base.
To do this you will need to use your existing skills, and maybe learn some new ones too.

● On task 1 Develop your design

On design sheet **3a** make a careful drawing of your final design idea. Use a ruler and other drawing aids to make it as neat as possible.

Remember the design must hold A6 paper (105 x 148mm) and be no bigger than 170 x 220mm.

DESIGN SHEET **3a**

A6 paper

148mm
220mm

105mm
170mm

Safety rules OK?

Workshops can be dangerous places.

Here are five simple rules to remember:

1. Never run.

2. Never use a tool without permission.

3. Always keep tools in the centre of the bench when not in use.

4. Always keep hair and clothing neatly tied back.

5. Always wear an apron, strong shoes and other protective devices when using tools.

On file

You will need a piece of **MDF (medium density fibreboard)**, plywood or acrylic. It should measure 170 mm **x** 220 mm.

The first skill that you will learn is filing. Your teacher will demonstrate how to file down to a line.

Make sure you make the edges of your base-board as straight as you can. This will make it easy for you to mark out and drill any holes you need accurately, even if your final design is curved or irregular.

To draw a straight, accurate line on your material, you will need to use a pencil and a ruler or try square.

Put your base-board in a vice while you file down to the pencil line with a flat file.

Each corner must be 90 degrees. Check this with a try square.

Files come in different shapes and sizes. Which one do you need?

End view   Plan view

● On task 2 Plan the making

On design sheet **3b** name the tools which you need to use for filing to a line and label them.
Explain what each is used for and how to use them safely.

On your design sheets

- Make a neat drawing of your final design idea. **3a**

- Name the tools that you need to use when marking out and filing to a straight line. **3b**

- Write down what each is used for and how to use it safely. **3b**

Remember

- You must always mark out accurately before shaping your material.

- Be aware of how to use tools safely. If you do not know, ask.

Skills with Drills

The next stage is to drill a hole in your base for a keyhole slot. This is so that the message pad holder can be hung up.

First you will need a drawing to show the position of the hole. It is important that your work is accurate. If not, your message pad holder will not hang straight!

● *On task 1 Work with materials*

1. On design sheet **4a** draw a rectangle 170 mm wide by 220 mm high.

2. Mark 15 mm down each side from the top of the rectangle with a feint dot.

3. Draw a line to join the two dots.

4. To find the centre of the line, measure 85 mm along the line from one side of the rectangle and mark with a vertical line.

You have now clearly marked where the centre of the hanging hole will be.

A little bit about drills

Drills are used to make round holes in wood, metal and plastics. There are several different types of drill you might use in the workshop.

This is a hand drill.

▷ Always make sure the drill is held tightly in the chuck.

▷ Try to keep the drill vertical.

Chuck

Jaws

Drill bit

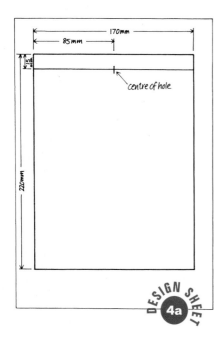

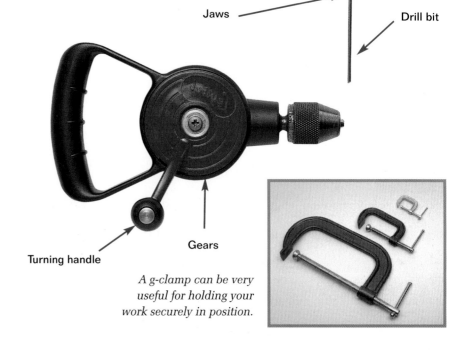

Turning handle

Gears

A g-clamp can be very useful for holding your work securely in position.

You may be able to use a hand-held power drill, or a floor or bench-top mounted pillar drill, like the one shown below.

Make sure you follow the specific safety instructions your teacher gives you.

Turning this handle brings the drill down to your work.

Make sure your work is securely fixed to the drilling table.

Place some scrap material under your work to protect the surface of the table.

Use this handle to raise the table closer to the drill.

On task 2 Work with materials

1. Mark out your base in the same way as you did on design sheet **4a**. Your teacher will demonstrate how to drill a 5 mm hole.

2. When you have finished drilling the hole, use a small round file to file out the top of the drilled hole to make an upside down *keyhole* shape.

$\varnothing$ 10 mm

Drill bits come in different diameters $\varnothing$.

You need to choose exactly the right one. It's a good idea to drill into a piece of scrap wood first to check the size of the hole.

On task 3 Plan the making

On design sheet **4b** draw a step-by-step plan of making an accurate *keyhole* slot, including safety precautions.   Why do you think that the hanging slot is this shape?

① Make sure the work is firmly held.

② Make sure I have some scrap wood to drill into.

③ Make sure the drill bit is firmly held in the chuck.

④ Keep my hands away from the drill bit.

Problems

I had problems when I measured from the end of the ruler and not the beginning of the scale. The hole ended up in the wrong place.

On your design sheets

- Make an accurate measured drawing of the position of the *keyhole* slot. **4a**
- Write a step by step plan of drilling a hole, including safety precautions. **4b**
- Write about any problems you had when marking out and drilling your hole. Explain how you solved them. **4b**

Remember

- You need to be accurate when you shape and form materials.
- Measured drawings and careful marking out will help you to be accurate.
- Always work safely.

Shape Up and Cut it Out

5

Get the Message?

Your message pad holder is now ready for shaping. To do this you will need to make a template and then cut out the shape with a saw.

Making a template

Go back to design sheet **3a**. Remind yourself what your final design looks like.

Before you start to shape your base you will need to make an accurate template of your final design. You can use this to draw around on your material. It is a quick and easy way to mark out the final shape of your base.

Draw template onto card

Check that paper fits

Cut template out

Place on wooden base and draw round it

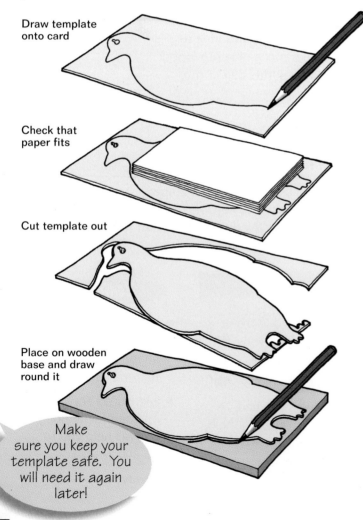

Make sure you keep your template safe. You will need it again later!

● On task 1 Develop your design

1. Draw your template onto card. It should be based on your final design.

2. Before you cut out your template check that the pad of paper (A6) will fit onto your base design.

3. Make sure that the template is accurate. Have you shown the position of the keyhole slot that you have already drilled?

4. When you are sure that your template is accurate, cut it out and place it onto your base. Then draw around it.

How are you coping so far?

You are now ready to cut out the final shape of your base-board. You will need to use a **tenon saw** and a **coping saw** for this.

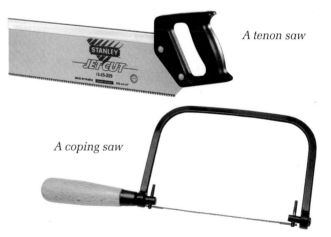

A tenon saw

A coping saw

Your teacher will demonstrate how to use:

▷ a tenon saw to cut straight lines and
▷ a coping saw to cut curves and holes.

Watch carefully!

PENCIL

RULER

DRILL

Go with the flow

Your next task is to draw a
flow diagram showing which
tools you need to use to shape
your base, and in which order.

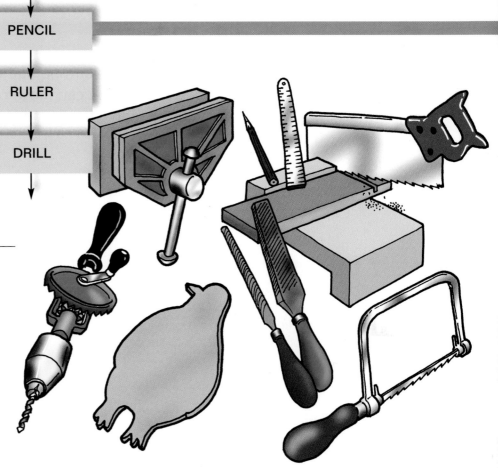

● On task 2 Plan the making

1. Decide which tools you will need to
   use and in what order. On design
   sheet **5** write down their names in a
   list in the order in which you will be
   using them.

2. Draw a box for each tool and write
   the name of the tool inside it.

3. Link the boxes with arrows to show
   the order in which the tools will be
   used.

4. Make notes about the safety
   precautions you have to take when
   cutting out the base-board.

● On task 3 Work with materials

Now cut out your base-board and finish the edges.
Remember to work safely at all times.

● On task 4 Apply what you know

On design sheet **5** make notes about any problems
you had while cutting the base out. How did you solve
them?

Problems and Solutions

DESIGN SHEET 5

Problem 1
The coping saw kept getting stuck in the
M.D.F. and I could not follow the line very
well.

Solution
My teacher told me to keep the coping saw
moving and to not press so hard. You can
also change the angle of the blade in the
frame to make following the line easier.

On your design sheets

- Draw a flow diagram of the tools
  you need to use to shape your
  base. **5**

- Make notes about the safety
  precautions you took. **5**

- Describe any problems you
  had while cutting out your
  base-board, and how you solved
  them. **5**

Remember

- If your message pad
  holder is going to be
  a successful product,
  your template needs
  to be accurate.

Hang On

6

Get the Message?

When you have completed the cutting out and shaping of your base-board you can move on to the next stage: adding the holding device and applying a perfect finish.

● **On task 1 Plan the making**

How will your holding device be attached to your base?

On design sheet **6a** show how you will fix the holding device to the base. Use pictures and words to show each stage.

● **On task 2 Work with materials**

Attach your holding device as you planned on design sheet **6a**.

The perfect finish

There are two main reasons for applying a finish to your work:

▷ to make your product look attractive

▷ to protect it when it is being used.

Your teacher will tell you what finishes you can use and show you how to use them. Remember that careless work at this stage can spoil the look of your product.

There are many different sorts of finishes. Varnishes come in a wide variety of colours. The majority come under the headings of **paints**, **varnishes** and **wood stains**. Sometimes wood stains and varnishes are combined in one product. Varnishes allow the grain or texture of the material to show through but paint completely covers the texture.

What are you going to use to apply your finish with?

● On task 3 Apply what you know

On design sheet **6b** write down the name of the finish that you are going to use on your base board. Explain how you are going to apply your finish.

● On task 4 Work with materials

Apply your chosen finish to a scrap of material first. Are you happy with the result? If so, take your time to carefully apply it to your message pad holder.

● On task 5 Evaluate

Go back to design sheet **6b** and make notes about any problems you had with attaching the holding device to the base or with adding a finish. Explain how you tried to solve the problems.

Problems and Solutions

DESIGN SHEET **6b**

Problem 2
When I painted my back board, the paint would not stick to the area where glue had spread from under the peg.

Solution
I should have wiped away the glue before it dried. There is nothing I can do to change this now.

On your design sheets

● Plan out how you are going to add a holding device to your message pad holder. **6a**

● Write down the name of the finish and how you are going to use it. **6b**

● Make notes about any problems that you had attaching the holding device, or adding a finish. **6b**

Remember

● Try out the chosen finish on scrap material before applying it to your finished product.

● Follow instructions carefully.

Finishing Off

7

Get the Message?

Finally, you need to look carefully at your finished product and evaluate it. Think carefully about its good and its less good points.

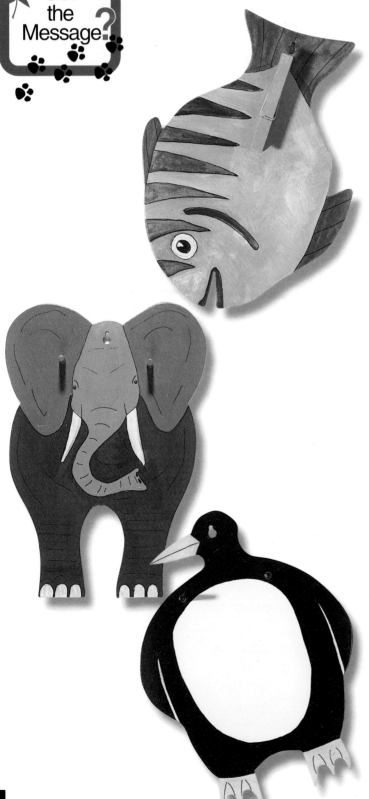

● *On task 1 Final evaluation*

On design sheet **7a** make a list of things that you think are important features of a message pad holder. For example, the way it looks and the way it works.

Message Pad - Important Features

① Is it well made?

② Is it well finished?

③ Does it hold enough paper?

DESIGN SHEET **7a**

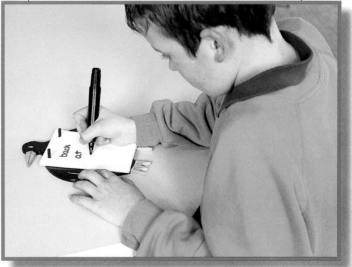

26

● On task 2 Final evaluation

1. Compare your list of important features with those chosen by the rest of your group. Working as a group, choose six important features.

2. On design sheet **7a**, write down the six features that your group have chosen.

3. Add a grid with the names of each person in your group, or use ICT to create a spreadsheet.

4. Working as a group, score each of your message pad holders out of 5 for each feature.

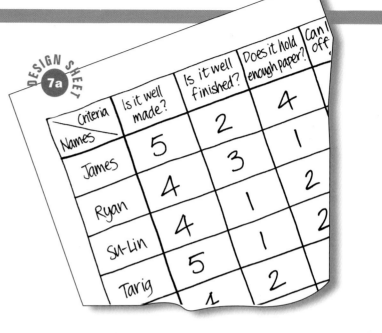

DESIGN SHEET **7a**

Criteria / Names	Is it well made?	Is it well finished?	Does it hold enough paper?	Can it... off...
James	5	2	4	
Ryan	4	3	1	2
Su-Lin	4	1	1	2
Tarig	5	2		
	4			

DESIGN SHEET **7b**

An idea for an additional feature

extra hole for left or right handed use

● On task 3 Final evaluation

On design sheet **7b**, write a few sentences in answer to the following questions:

▶ How well does your own message pad holder measure up to the features your group identified as being important?

▶ How could you improve your score for each of the features if you were going to make the message pad holder again?

▶ What additional features might improve your product? Write down ideas for adding additional features, such as a pen holder. Sketch what the message pad holder would look like with the improvements in place.

On your design sheets

● List the important features of a message pad holder. **7a**

● Draw up a grid or spreadsheet to show the findings of the group evaluation of the message pad holders. **7a**

● Write about how well your product scored. How could you improve its score? Write and draw ideas for adding other features to your message pad holder. **7b**

Remember

● When you have finished making your product, you must evaluate it and suggest how it could be improved.

Starting Point

A high street shop sells products from around the world. It wants to boost its sales during the autumn and winter months. Can you design a new decorative product for them to sell?

Most of the world's religions have festivals of light. Light is seen as a symbol of goodness, a force against the powers of darkness and evil. As the days grow shorter and the nights longer, our human response to darkness is to celebrate light.

Menorah, Jewish lights

Hindu festival, India

Hanukkah, festival of lights

Mid-autumn lantern festival, Hong Kong

Christmas tree

A Cunning Plan

2

All Fall Down

3

6

5

4

Nearly Finished

One Small Step

Lighting Up

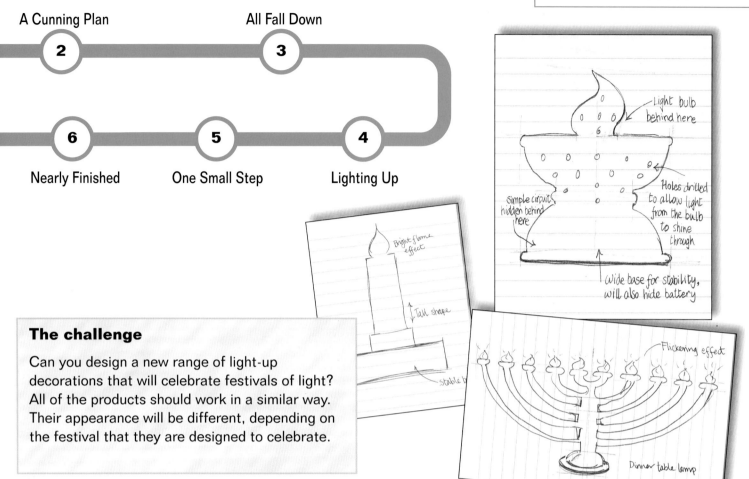

The challenge

Can you design a new range of light-up decorations that will celebrate festivals of light? All of the products should work in a similar way. Their appearance will be different, depending on the festival that they are designed to celebrate.

The shop owner has provided you with the sketches shown above. These show the kind of product they are looking for.

The product should be based on the theme of festivals of light from around the world. To make it more attractive it should include a battery-operated light source.

● On task Apply what you know

Use your own personal knowledge of a festival of light to write a short description of how it is celebrated.

► Who is involved?

► What does each person do?

► Do you have special food?

► Are there special rituals to celebrate the festival?

► Are there any decorations or objects that only appear at that time of year?

Illustrate your writing with drawings. Use design sheet **1a**.

The focus

In this project you will work with a range of materials, adhesives and electrical components. You will learn how to measure, cut and join materials accurately. You will also learn how to make stable structures and build simple circuits.

The end product

You will design and make a decoration to celebrate your chosen festival of light. Here is a list of design requirements. To be successful the product must:

► be designed to appeal to your target market

► celebrate a festival of light

► be stable

► work reliably

► look attractive

► be between 150 mm and 200 mm high.

Festivals of Light

1

Making Light Work

First of all you need to decide who your product is aimed at. Then you can find out what might appeal to them.

Every Buddhist country has its own festival of light. In Thailand, the festival is celebrated by floating thousands of candles down rivers and streams as an offering to the spirits of the rivers.

Aiming for the target market

If your product is going to be successful, you will need to think carefully about:

▷ who might buy it
▷ how you are going to make it appeal to them.

The people that you aim your product at are called the **target market**.

You will need to consider whether you are going to make a product that will appeal to:

▷ a wide number of different groups or
▷ a single group of people.

For example, Hanukkah is celebrated by lighting candles on an eight-branched candlestick. However this design might not appeal to, for example, the Hindu community. At the same time, a Christmas tree may not appeal to a family celebrating Hanukkah.

This limits the number of people who might buy the product. Can you design something that will appeal to more than one culture?

What shapes might be acceptable to Hindus, Sikhs, Jews, Buddhists and Christians? What shapes and colours do any of them have in common?

Sikhs celebrate Diwali. It marks three key events in the history of Sikhism. Can you find out what these are? Houses are spring cleaned ready for the winter and candles and fireworks are lit.

The Hindu festival of light is also called Diwali. It is the most widely celebrated Hindu festival. The word Diwali means garland of light. Traditionally houses were decorated with divas, little clay bowls which burned oil. Now electric lights are often used.

● *On task 1 Investigate*

1. Decide on your target market. Write this down on design sheet **1b**.

2. Investigate the festivals of light of the faith or faiths of your chosen target market. Make sure you find out about the symbols connected with these festivals. You will need these for your designs. Make notes about where you are going to look for this information. As well as using books and other printed sources, use the Internet and CD-ROMs. Your RE teacher or local religious leaders in your community may be able to help.

3. Record what you find out on design sheet **1b**. Include drawings, photocopies and pictures downloaded from the Internet. Say where you found your information.

Hanukkah is the Jewish festival. It marks a special occasion in Jewish history. Try to find out about this. The special canlestick that is used at Hanukkah is called the Hanukkiyah.

Advent candles are lit during the Christian festival of Christmas. The festival celebrates the birth of Christ. The candle represents His light coming into the world. The Christmas tree has non-Christian or even Pagan origins, but is still used to celebrate the festival.

● **On task 2 Investigate**

1. Look back at the design requirements listed under the heading *The end product* on page 29. Write them down on design sheet **1c**.

2. Add to these requirements your own list of features that your product will need to have. These must be based on what you have found out about your target market.

Design checklist

The original design requirements and the ones you have added make up your **design checklist**. As you develop your ideas keep looking at your checklist to make sure your designs do all of these things.

● **On task 3 Have good ideas**

On design sheet **1d** draw some initial ideas for shapes that you can use, based on the information that you have gathered. Remember that it must be between 150 mm and 200 mm high.

DESIGN SHEET **1d**

Shapes I could use

On your design sheets

- Write down and illustrate information about the faith or faiths whose festival of light you have chosen to investigate. **1b**

- Write a list of the features that your product will need to have, based on what you have found out about your target market. **1c**

- Draw a variety of ideas for shapes that you could use. **1d**

Remember

- The people that your product is aimed at are called the target market.

- Think carefully about who will buy your product and how you are going to make it appeal to them.

31

A Cunning Plan

2

Working drawings of new designs are usually done in orthographic projection. Another way to show your ideas is by isometric drawings.

Orthographic drawings

Plans are drawn from a **bird's eye view**, that is looking straight down from above. They only show the length and width of something, not its height. They don't show what the sides look like.

Elevations are very similar to plans. They only show two dimensions of something – the length and height, or the width and height. They do show what the sides look like, but not the top.

If a plan and two elevations are drawn side-by-side, the three drawings will together show the length, width and height.

The position of the two drawings is very important. They need to line up exactly. These are known as **orthographic** drawings. Look closely at the drawings below. Use a ruler to see how the various parts of the plan and elevations all line up.

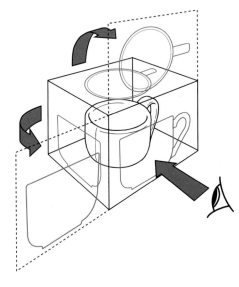

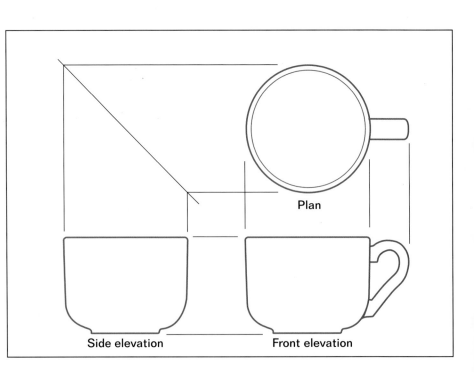

Plan

Side elevation   Front elevation

Isometric drawing

When drawing in **isometric** all the vertical lines are drawn vertically. The horizontal lines (that is those that show width and depth) are drawn at 30 degrees.

You can use printed underlay sheets to help you draw in isometric. You need to use a sheet of thin paper or layout paper, so you can see the printed grid underneath.

To produce an accurate isometric drawing you need to use a 30°/60° set square and either a parallel motion drawing board or a T-square.

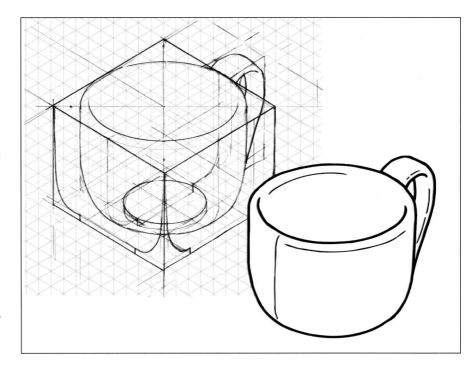

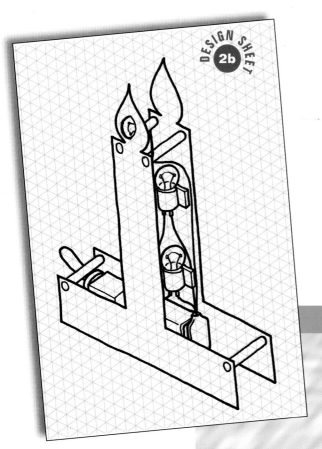

DESIGN SHEET 2b

● **On task**
Apply what you know / Develop your design

1. Choose three different objects. Make sure you have them in front of you – don't try to work from memory. Draw the plans and elevations for each of them on design sheet **2a**. Remember to ensure they line up in the correct way.

2. If you have access to a computer, try drawing your plans and elevations on screen.

3. Try drawing some ideas for your decorative product in isometric on design sheet **2b**. Remember that your product will need a back as well as a front. Show where the light bulbs, the battery and the switch might be placed.

On your design sheets

● Draw plans and elevations for three objects. **2a**

● Develop your design using 3D sketches. **2b**

Remember

● Plan and elevation drawings are combined together to produce orthographic drawings.

● Isometric drawings show what an object looks like in 3D.

All Fall Down

3

Your product will need to stand safely and securely on a table or other surface, for example a window sill or mantelshelf. On this page is some information that will help you to achieve this.

What do you know about designing structures?

What is a structure?

Look around you and you will see many examples of structures. **Structures** are found in nature and in products that have been made.

A structure needs to support itself and the load or force that is put on it. For example, a chair needs to be able to support itself and the person who sits on it. A flower stalk needs to support both itself and the flower.

Frame structures

Frame structures are made up of several parts or members. Many frame structures are stabilised by **triangulation**. By adding an extra member across a rectangle, the structure is made more stable.

Shell structures

Shell structures are made from a continuous *skin*. The shape of the structure provides its strength. These structures are sometimes called **monocoques**.

Many structures are a **combination** of frame and shell structures.

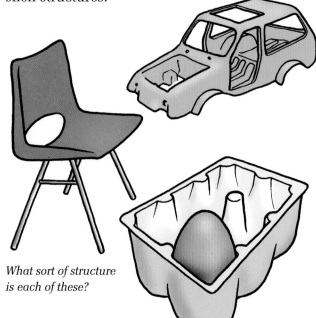

What sort of structure is each of these?

Stable structures

When a structure cannot support both itself and the load or force on it, it breaks. This is called **structural failure**. When a structure balances external forces and internal forces, it is in **equilibrium** and we say it is **stable**.

It is essential that the structures in a bridge and the forces acting on it are in equilibrium.

Galloping Gertie was a bridge over the Tacoma Narrows in the USA. The bridge could not support itself, the cars going over it and also the force of the 67 k.p.h. winds. It was not in equilibrium when it broke up.

Centre of gravity

Another way of stabilising structures is to give them a low centre of gravity. To do this they need to have a wide base or have most of the weight of the object towards its base. This means that they will not easily topple over.

● *On task* **Apply what you know / Have good ideas**

1. Look carefully at the illustrations above. How has each structure been stabilised?

Draw the four structures on design sheet **3a**. Label each one with notes about how you think it has been stabilised.

2. Look back at your designs. Your product will be placed flat on a surface. Sketch your idea on design sheet **3b** and add notes to explain what methods you will use to make it stable.

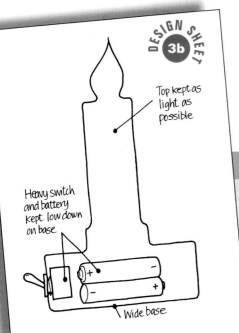

DESIGN SHEET **3b**

Top kept as light as possible

Heavy switch and battery kept low down on base

Wide base

On your design sheets

- Draw four examples of structures and make notes on the drawings about how each has been stabilised. **3a**

- Draw a diagram and make notes about how you think your decoration will be stabilised. **3b**

Remember

- A structure needs to be able to support itself and the load or force that is put on it.

- When a structure balances external and internal forces, it is in equilibrium.

- Triangulation and a low centre of gravity are used to make structures more stable.

Lighting Up

4

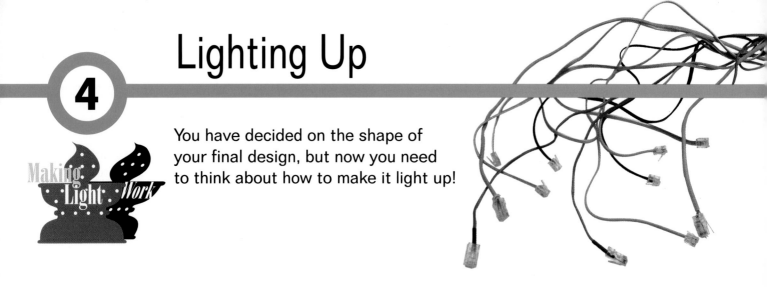

You have decided on the shape of your final design, but now you need to think about how to make it light up!

Here we go round

Electrical current will only flow around a complete circuit without any breaks. Its flow can be turned on and off using a switch. The switch makes a break in the circuit.

Electronic devices are made up from a small number of different **components**. Each one does a particular job.

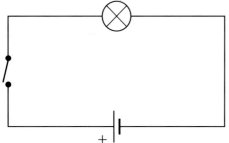

A simple circuit showing a bulb, switch and battery.

Light emitting diodes (LEDs)

You could use an LED. LEDs use a very small electrical current. A battery will therefore last a long time.

LEDs should not be connected directly to a battery. A protective fixed resistor should be used with the LED. They also need to be connected the correct way: the short leg to +ve and the long leg to –ve.

470R

A circuit showing an LED, resistor and battery.

Resistors are useful

The rate at which the current flows around a circuit can be changed by using **resistors**.

If the circuit that you are making for your product has LEDs (light emitting diodes), you will need to restrict the flow of electricity to them using resistors.

Their values are measured in ohms. The symbol for ohms is Ω, for example: $2.7\,\Omega$, $330\,\Omega$ and $4700\,\Omega$.

Fixed resistors have three coloured bands around them. Each colour stands for a number. By working out the numbers you can work out the value of the resistor.

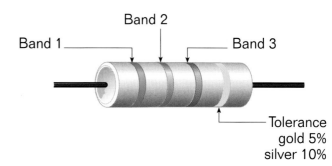

Band 2

Band 1

Band 3

Tolerance
gold 5%
silver 10%

Colour	Band 1	Band 2	Band 3
Black	–	0	None
Brown	1	1	0
Red	2	2	00
Orange	3	3	000
Yellow	4	4	0000
Green	5	5	000000
Blue	6	6	0000000
Violet	7	7	–
Grey	8	8	–
White	9	9	–
Gold	–	–	0.1
Silver	–	–	0.01

Soldering on

Before you solder your circuit, check with your drawing to ensure you have the components in the correct place.

▷ Ensure all the components are clean.
  Try not to touch the areas to be soldered.

▷ Heat the components and copper track if you are using it.

▷ Allow a small amount of solder to melt between the components and track.

▷ Remove the solder wire.

▷ Remove the soldering iron and trim any component legs.

You will need to use a pair of pliers as a heat sink because LEDs are sensitive to heat.

Electronic symbols

Each different electronic component can be represented in a drawing by its own symbol. Try to get into the habit of using these symbols when designing circuits.

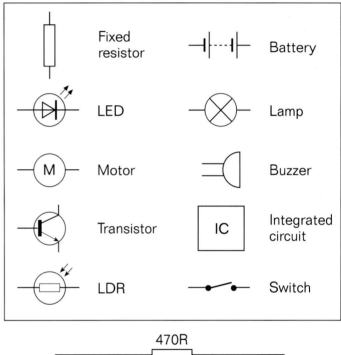

	Fixed resistor		Battery
	LED		Lamp
	Motor		Buzzer
	Transistor	IC	Integrated circuit
	LDR		Switch

470R

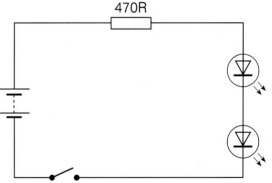

Even if you are using two LEDs you only need one resistor.

● On task Investigate

Find three products LEDs have been used in. Draw these products on design sheet **4**. Explain what function the LED performs.

On your design sheet

● Draw three products that use LEDs. Describe what the LEDs do. **4**

Remember

● Always check your circuit against your drawing before you solder the components in place.

One Small Step

5

You have finalised your idea and made a template of your design. Next you must write down detailed information about the finished product to help you to make it exactly right.

Product specification

When you have decided on your final design, you need to think about writing a specification for your product. This will include very detailed information about the finished product.

If someone else was to make your design for you, the specification and drawings would help to make sure that the finished product was exactly what you had designed.

Here are some points to consider for your specification:

▷ the size of the decoration

▷ the materials it will be made from

▷ joining methods to be used

▷ components to be used

▷ finishes to be used.

These details will help you to plan the making of your product.

● On task 1 Apply what you know

On design sheet **5a** write a specification for your product. You might want to use the list on the right, to start you off. There may be other things that you have thought about.

DESIGN SHEET 5a

Specification

Candle size – 180mm high
150mm wide at base

Materials used – M.D.F. back
Acrylic front
Wooden dowels

Components – 2 x 1·5v batteries
1 x Battery holder
1 x Battery holder cap
4 x 1·5v bulbs
4 x Bulb holders
1 x Toggle switch

GLOSS PAINT 1 LITRE

Plan the making

When you make your product, you will have to make sure that you do not make any mistakes in the order in which you do things. To stop this from happening you need to plan the making.

● *On task 2 Plan the making*

Below is a list of some of the things that you are likely to need to do to make your product. They are not in the correct order.

Rearrange and re-write them as necessary on design sheet **5b** so that they are a list of instructions for how to make your product. If any steps have been left out, add them to the plan.

▶ Use the template to mark out the design onto acrylic.
▶ Attach the circuit to the MDF using a glue gun. (Make sure you can get to the switch easily when the acrylic front is in position.)
▶ Cut around each shape using a coping saw.
▶ Finish the edges using glasspaper and files.
▶ Tape the two shapes together.
▶ Paint both sides of the MDF and leave to dry.
▶ Drill small holes in the acrylic to let the light shine through.
▶ Use the template to mark out the design onto MDF.
▶ Push the acrylic front of the decoration onto the dowels.
▶ Paint the dowels to match the acrylic front.
▶ Switch on, stand back and enjoy it!
▶ Drill four holes the right size for the dowels: at the top left and top right, and at the bottom left and bottom right.
▶ Glue dowels into the holes in the MDF.

Planning the Making

① Use the template to mark out the design onto acrylic
② Use the template to mark out th design onto M.D.F.
③ Cut out around each shape using a coping saw
④ ...pe the two shapes toge...
⑤ ...inish the edges usin... and files
⑥ Drill holes the rig... two at the top, ... at the bottom

Remember

● Write a specification detailing exactly what you are going to make and how you are going to make it before you start making.

● It is very important that you plan the main steps of manufacture before you start making.

On your design sheets

● Write a specification for your product. **5a**

● List the steps of making your product in the correct order. **5b**

Nearly Finished

6

Now you are ready to start making your product. First you need to know more about finishes and adhesives.

Fine finishes

A **file** is used to straighten and finish the edges of most materials. A file will be useful for this project. You will also need to use glasspaper, which does a similar job.

Glasspaper can be used for awkward areas that the file cannot reach into, as well as being used to finish a large, flat surface. It comes in a range of different grades. It is sometimes called sandpaper.

Glasspaper should be used to remove pencil marks. Never use an eraser as this can leave a fine film of rubber, making it difficult to apply an even finish to your material.

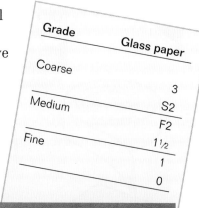

Grade	Glass paper
Coarse	
	3
Medium	S2
	F2
Fine	1½
	1
	0

Paint

You will need to apply a finish to your product. If you are using MDF, paint will be the most suitable finish. If you are using timber, you could use varnish, stain or paint. Your teacher will tell you what is available for you to use.

Below are some important points to remember when using paint.

▷ There are three main types of paint: oil based paint, polyurethane paint and enamel paint.

▷ Surfaces to be painted should be lightly sanded.

▷ They should be clean and free from dust.

▷ Some paints are able to give a very good finish with only one coat, others need two or more thin coats.

▷ If you use a spray paint, you must wear a mask.

▷ Always read the manufacturer's instructions.

Let's stick together

You will need to use a strong adhesive when you glue the dowels into the holes in the MDF. You do not want them to come loose when you take the acrylic front off to change the battery or bulbs.

You need to choose carefully. On the right is a chart to help you.

Adhesive	Example	Appearance/properties
PVA	Resin W	Thick, white liquid
Contact adhesive	Thixofix	Thick, rubbery glue
Rubber solution	Bostick	Clear, rubbery glue
Hot glue	Bostick	Solid when cold, liquid when hot

Glue gun

A **glue gun** is a tool which can be very useful, but needs to be carefully handled as it can be very hot and dangerous to use.

It works by passing cold, solid glue sticks over a heating element using a trigger in the handle. Hot, melted glue comes out of the nozzle at one end of the glue gun.

Glue sticks come in a range of types for use with different materials, as well as a general purpose type.

Remember

- Make sure that surfaces to be painted are smooth, clean and free from dust.

- The adhesive you use must be the right one for the materials you are joining together.

● *On task Work with materials*

1. On design sheet **6**, explain which finishes you will use. Say how you will apply them to your product.

2. Also on design sheet **6**, explain which type of adhesive you will use, and say why.

On your design sheet

- Explain which finishes and adhesives you are going to use and why. **6**

Celebrate Your Success

7

Flick the switch and let your decoration shine!

You have worked hard to get this far. Now you need to think about how well you have designed and made your product.

Check it out!

On page 29 the design requirements for a successful product were listed. The decoration had to:

▷ appeal to your target market.

▷ celebrate a festival of light

▷ be stable

▷ work reliably

▷ look attractive

▷ be between 150 mm and 200 mm high.

These are the things that you had to think about while you were designing.

Does your finished product do each of these?

On page 31 you added some further requirements of your own on design sheet **1c**.

Does your finished product do each of these as well?

● On task 1 Final evaluation

1. Check each of the items on your design checklist to see if your product is successful. To help do this try making each of the items into a question. For example: Is my product stable?

2. Write down each question on design sheet **7a** and answer it. If you answer no to any of them, you need to explain why.

● On task 2 Final evaluation

1. Swap your product and design checklist with a partner who designed their product for a similar target market.

2. Compare your design checklists and discuss how the requirements influenced your decisions about what your design would be like. Record this on design sheet **7a**.

3. Write a short report that compares the products you evaluated. Include comments about how well they have been made as well as how well they have been designed. Do this on design sheet **7b**.

DESIGN SHEET 7b

Jane's Christmas tree is more stable than Edward's candle because he put the switch too high up the candle, making it wobble.

Reporting back

● *On task 3 Final evaluation*

1. On design sheet **7c** evaluate your own making process. Write down any problems that you had during each of the following stages of making your decoration and explain how you solved them:

▶ cutting out the shapes in MDF and acrylic

▶ making the circuit

▶ applying the finish to the MDF

▶ assembling the decoration.

2. What ideas have you got for improvements to your design? Show these on design sheet **7d**.

DESIGN SHEET 7a

It works reliably and it is stable. It looks attractive because there are lots of holes for the light to shine through.

You can easily get to the switch to turn it on and off.

On your design sheets

● Write down whether your product meets each of the original design criteria. **7a**

● Write a short report about someone else's product. **7b**

● Evaluate how well you made your product. **7c**

● Show your ideas for improving your design. **7d**

DESIGN SHEET 7c

Evaluation:
How well did I make my product?

I did not find it very easy to cut out the acrylic so the finish on the edge is not very good.

It was easier to cut the M.D.F. and I am pleased that the two pieces are the same size and shape.

The finish on the acrylic is better than the finish on the M.D.F. as I could not match the colours properly.

Remember

● Use your design checklist to evaluate your decoration to see if it is successful.

● Evaluate both the finished product and the making process. That way you can learn from your mistakes.

Starting Point

We all spend a lot of time travelling, to school, to work or on holiday. Sometimes we can get bored. There are many ways of passing the time. These include playing games and doing puzzles.

Can you design and make a travel game that would help pass the time while travelling?

The market for toys and games is enormous. Toys and games that are linked to other products and services are even more profitable.

A toy manufacturer wants you to design and make a simple travel game. It should be based on the idea of a series of marbles or steel balls falling into holes in a maze.

The manufacturer hopes to encourage other companies and organisations to add their own name and logo to it to use as a form of advertising. This type of promotion is called **merchandising**.

Have you ever been lost in a maze?

The maze at Hampton Court Palace was designed in 1690

The Arkville maze.

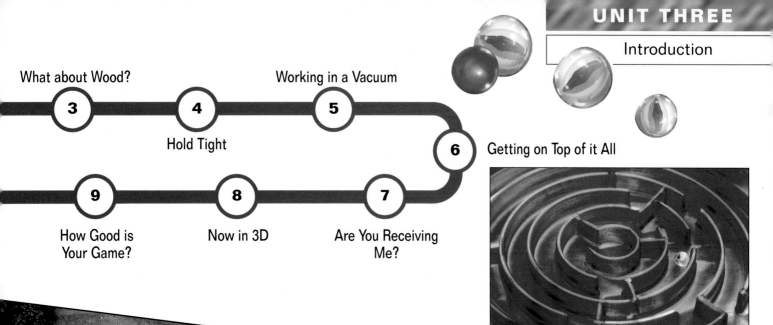

What about Wood? **3** — **4** — Working in a Vacuum **5**

Hold Tight

6 Getting on Top of it All

9 — **8** — **7**

How Good is Your Game? Now in 3D Are You Receiving Me?

The Lappa maze in the shape of Trevithick's locomotive.

The challenge

You have been asked to design and make a simple travel game. To do this you will need to take some careful decisions about:

▶ what type of maze game to develop

▶ the visual theme of the game

▶ the size of the design.

The focus

In this unit you will focus on working with wood and plastic. You will gain skills and experience in how they can be cut and joined.

You will also find out how plastic can be formed into a complex shape using a vacuum former.

As part of the project you will learn how computers can be used to help us design and make things. This is called CAD/CAM.

The end product

You will design and make a travel game. To be successful it must:

▶ appeal to teenagers

▶ promote a company or person, such as a sportswear manufacturer or a pop group.

Sell, Sell, Sell

1

Amazing Mazes

The names and faces of the famous are often used to increase sales of a product.

Which pop groups, film stars or sporting personalities are teenagers most interested in?

Start your investigation by finding out how companies use famous people and images to help sell products.

Pop, movies or sport?

Famous pop, movie and sporting stars are always in the public's view. They earn large amounts of money by endorsing certain products. For example, a sportswear company will pay a famous sporting star to wear the company's clothing.

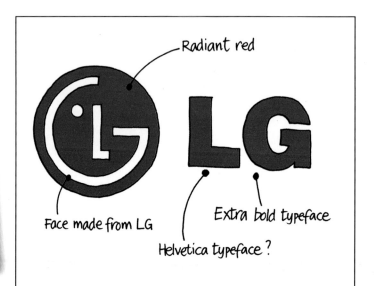

- Radiant red
- Face made from LG
- Helvetica typeface?
- Extra bold typeface

Michael Owen's football boot.

● On task 1 Investigate

1. On design sheet **1a** list ten famous pop, movie or sporting stars. Say what each one is famous for.

2. Find photographs of at least one of these stars. Fix these onto design sheet **1a**.

3. Choose a well-known company that might wish to have their logo or symbol on the game. Make a neat copy of their logo on design sheet **1b**.

   ▶ Check the sizes of each element.

   ▶ Match the colours as closely as possible.

   ▶ Can you find out the names of any typefaces used? Try looking at the typefaces available on a word-processing or graphics computer program.

You will be using the star and/or company you have illustrated on design sheets **1a** and **1b** on your maze game.

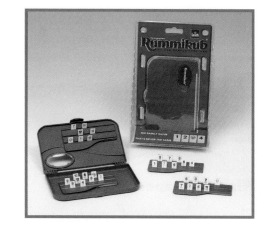

Existing solutions

You can learn a lot from studying existing travel games:

▷ How well do they cater for the needs of the people who use them?

▷ What shape and size are they?

▷ How are they carried when not in use?

▷ What materials are they made from, and why?

▷ How might they have been assembled?

● **On task 2 Evaluate**

1. Obtain a number of travel games.

2. On design sheet **1c** sketch one or more of them out. Add colour. Add notes to your sketch to answer the *Existing solutions* questions above.

3. Discuss your answers within your group. At the bottom of design sheet **1c** write down which game you think is the best design, and why.

5. Write a list of the best features of the games you looked at. Should any of these features be included in your design?

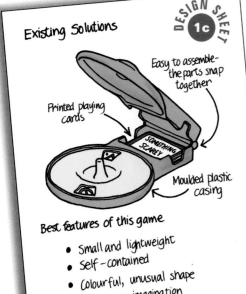

DESIGN SHEET **1c**

Existing Solutions

Easy to assemble – the parts snap together

Printed playing cards

Moulded plastic casing

Best features of this game
- Small and lightweight
- Self-contained
- Colourful, unusual shape
- Encourages imagination

On your design sheets

● Explain your choice of a famous person and find an image of them. **1a**

● Explain your choice of company that might want to put their logo on the product. **1b**

● Evaluate some existing travel games and write a list of their best features. **1c**

Remember

● You can learn a lot by studying products that have already been designed and made.

47

Shaping Up

2

Amazing Mazes

The next stage is to make some important decisions about the shape and size of your maze game.

Simple shapes

The outside shape of your maze game needs to be a simple symmetrical shape, such as a square or rectangle.

If you want to use a different shape keep the corners either 90 degrees or 45 degrees. This will make it easier to manufacture.

The outside shape could be based on a simple shape relating to the star or company you have chosen.

● On task 1 Have good ideas

On design sheet **2a**, draw a variety of shapes you could use for your game. Add colour to make the shapes stand out.

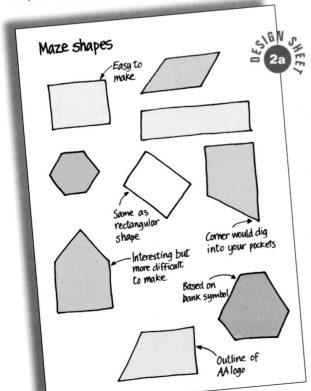

Pocket-sized?

Remember your game must be portable. It will need to fit into a school bag or pocket.

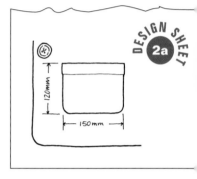

● On task 2 Investigate

1. Measure the size of all the pockets on your coat and in your school bag. Write these out in chart form on design sheet **2a**.

2. Think carefully about the maximum height, width and depth your game should be.

Are you losing your marbles?

The toy manufacturer wants you to design and make a game based on the idea of a ball rolling round a maze. You will need to decide what size of ball to use. A steel ball or marble would be suitable.

● On task 3 Investigate

Use calipers to measure accurately the diameter of the ball you have decided to use. Record what you discovered on design sheet **2b**.

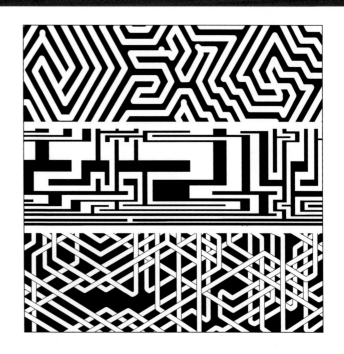

● On task 4 Develop your design

On design sheet **2b** write a design specification for your game. Focus on the main requirements. Make a statement about each of the following:

▶ what age group the game is intended for

▶ what sort of game it is

▶ which pop, movie or sports star and/or company will be represented

▶ what the maximum size of the base can be

▶ what size of ball is being used.

● On task 5 Have good ideas

Decide which shapes would be most suitable for the age group it is intended for. Re-draw them on design shet **2b** and add lines to show possible layouts of the maze. Consider where the start and finish will be.

● On task 6 Develop your design

1. Look at your range of ideas and talk to a friend about them. How well do they match your design specification? Discuss any problems there might be with any of them.

2. When you are happy with one of your ideas, draw a full size plan of it on design sheet **2c**. Remember to allow for the thickness of the materials that you will use for the maze and the outside case.

3. Check you leave enough space for the ball. Mark the start and finish. Show how the ball will be held in place at the start/finish.

DESIGN SHEET 2c

Finish →○

I must ensure that the ball will run through the maze OK

?○

Start ○

My teacher agreed that this maze design would be the best one to make as it was not too complicated

On your design sheets

● Sketch some possible shapes for your game. **2a**

● Show how you worked out the maximum size the game can be, and the size of the steel ball or marble. **2a**

● List the main requirements for your game. **2b**

● Draw a range of ideas and develop these into a final idea. **2b / 2c**

Remember

● Draw lots of ideas, don't try and come up with your final idea straight away.

● Think about size and ease of manufacture.

What about Wood?

Wood is an easy material to work with and to give a protective finish to. It is also comfortable and safe to hold.

What do you know about the many different types of wood that are available?

Softwoods and hardwoods

There are two main types of wood.

Hardwoods come from deciduous trees. These lose their leaves in winter. Examples include ash, oak and mahogany.

Softwoods come from coniferous trees. These keep their leaves in winter. Examples include pine and spruce.

Kelobra

Ash

Pearwood

Red cedar

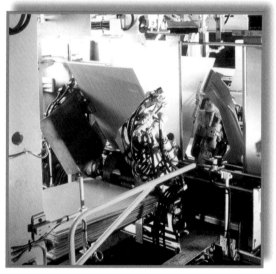

Manufacturing boards.

Manufactured boards

Manufactured boards are flat sheets of material made from natural timber. They are made from:

▷ thin sheets of wood that are glued together, or

▷ small particles of wood that are compressed together with glue.

The advantage of using this type of material is that it is available in large flat sheets that can be finished easily.

Examples of manufactured boards are plywood, chipboard, hardboard and medium density fibreboard (MDF).

Finishing

If wood is not protected it will deteriorate. You can use paint, dyes, stains or varnish to protect wood. This will also enhance its appearance. If the wood is to be left permanently outside then it is better to use a preservative.

To obtain a good quality finish the material must be carefully prepared first. It needs to be rubbed down using various grades of glass paper. Several coats of the finish may then need to be applied.

When designing products for children it is important to check that the finish is safe, that is, it is non-toxic.

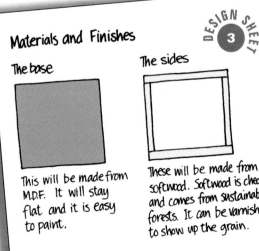

A new home in Thailand made from teak. Teak is a timber that has natural oil in it that helps protect it. Unfortunately, teak is expensive to use.

Materials and Finishes

DESIGN SHEET 3

The base

This will be made from M.D.F. It will stay flat and it is easy to paint.

The sides

These will be made from softwood. Softwood is cheap and comes from sustainable forests. It can be varnished to show up the grain.

The maze

The cover

Environmental Issues

Hardwoods

Many hardwoods come from tropical rain forests. It is important that these are not destroyed. For this reason companies are looking for materials that can be used instead of hardwood. A successful example is the use of PVC window frames.

Softwoods
Softwood is used to make paper and card products. The UK is self-sufficient in the use of softwood. This means that trees are replanted at the same rate as they are cut down. To help reduce the number of trees needed, we are now encouraged to recycle old newspapers and manufacturers use packaging made from recycled card.

● *On task Apply what you know*

1. On design sheet **3** state what type of wood you will be using for your game, and what finish you will use.

2. Make a statement about the environmental issues involved in the materials in your game.

On your design sheets

● Explain what materials and finishes you will be using in your game. **3**

● Discuss the impact on the environment of using these materials for your game. **3**

Remember

● There are two main types of wood. These are softwood and hardwood.

● Manufactured boards are made from sheets or particles of wood.

● All types of wood need to be correctly finished to protect them.

Hold Tight

Next you need to decide how to join the frame of your box together.

Joints and construction

There are a variety of joints you can use to make the sides of the box for your game. The type of joint you use may depend on the cross-sectional shape of the material.

Modern glues are very strong but a joint will help improve the strength of the game and hold the pieces in place while the glue dries. The joint increases the size of the gluing area.

Which joint would be most suitable for the sides of your box?

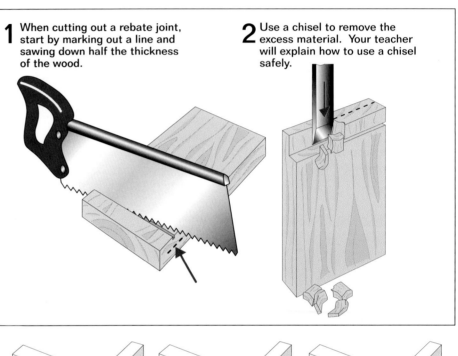

1 When cutting out a rebate joint, start by marking out a line and sawing down half the thickness of the wood.

2 Use a chisel to remove the excess material. Your teacher will explain how to use a chisel safely.

Butt joint	Finger joint	Rebate

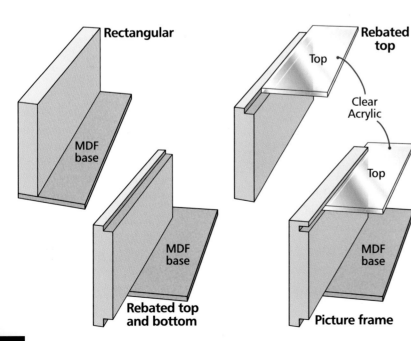

Rectangular

MDF base

MDF base

Rebated top and bottom

Rebated top

Top

Clear Acrylic

Top

MDF base

Picture frame

Cross-sectional shape

You can buy wood in a variety of cross-sectional shapes. This is called moulding. Some shapes are very detailed and can be used for picture frames. Ask your teacher to show you what shapes are available at your school.

Are any of these shapes suitable for the sides of your box?

● On task 1 Plan the making

Draw a plan of your maze game on design sheet **4**. Add dimensions. Say which sections and joints you will use. Explain the reasons for your choice.   For the base you should use thin sheet materials, such as 4mm thick MDF. Show how the base will be fitted.

● On task 2 Work with materials

1. Cut the sides and base for your game.

2. Carefully cut the joints and assemble the box. Keep checking the measurements and accuracy of the fit.

3. When the sides and base are finished, glue them together, as shown below.

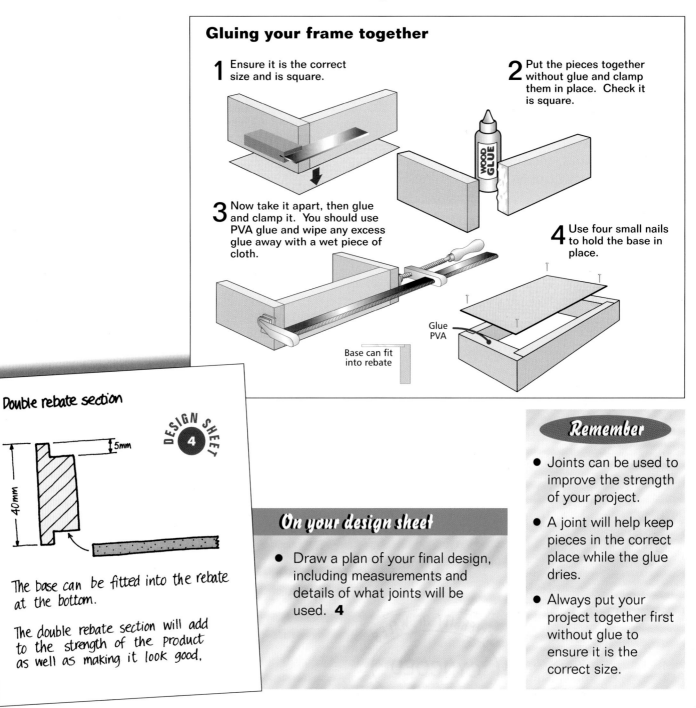

Gluing your frame together

1 Ensure it is the correct size and is square.

2 Put the pieces together without glue and clamp them in place. Check it is square.

3 Now take it apart, then glue and clamp it. You should use PVA glue and wipe any excess glue away with a wet piece of cloth.

4 Use four small nails to hold the base in place.

Glue PVA

Base can fit into rebate

Double rebate section

5mm

40mm

The base can be fitted into the rebate at the bottom.

The double rebate section will add to the strength of the product as well as making it look good.

DESIGN SHEET 4

On your design sheet

● Draw a plan of your final design, including measurements and details of what joints will be used. **4**

Remember

● Joints can be used to improve the strength of your project.

● A joint will help keep pieces in the correct place while the glue dries.

● Always put your project together first without glue to ensure it is the correct size.

Working in a Vacuum

5

Amazing Mazes

The maze itself will be made from plastic sheet, using a vacuum former.

Vacuum forming is a manufacturing process used to make identical copies of simple parts that need to have the same shape.

Types of plastic

There are two types of plastic:

▷ thermoplastic

▷ thermoset plastic.

Thermoplastics can be warmed and reshaped. **Thermoset plastics**, once moulded into shape, are set for good. Plastic can be clear or opaque in any colour.

Collections by Guido Cerere

Vacuum forming

Vacuum forming is used in industry to make many familiar products, such as egg boxes, baths and trays. It is a simple and cheap process and can be done in school.

The vacuum former uses thermoplastic in sheet form. Thermoplastic means its shape can be changed when it is warmed. When it is cooled the material stays in shape.

Thermoplastics that can be used include:
* polystyrene
* PVC (polyvinyl chloride)
* polypropylene
* acrylic.

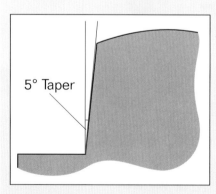

5° Taper

Only certain shapes can be made using a vacuum former. They need to be simple and have sloping sides.

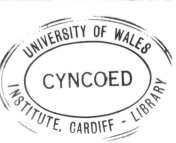

Making the mould

● On task 1 Plan the making

1. Draw the design of your maze full size. You could do this using CAD (Computer Aided Design). Remember that the outside shape and size of your maze must be the same as the inside shape of your case. Mark the start and finish of your maze on this drawing.

2. Read the process of making the mould outlined in On task 2 below. What parts of the making process do you think might cause problems? Make a note of these on design sheet **5**. What could you do about them? What special safety precautions will you need to take?

● On task 2 Work with materials

1. Cut a piece of MDF or plywood that is the same size as the inside of your case. Use this as a base to glue your design to.

2. Your teacher will give you some strips of wood that have been cut with a tapered side. You will use these to make the tracks on your mould. Cut them to the size of the track you intend to make.

3. Glue the tapered strips of wood to the base to make your mould. Check your marble will roll easily around the maze.

4. When the glue is dry, drill some small holes in the corners of the maze. These will ensure the plastic is sucked right down.

5. Vacuum form your maze. Carefully trim the moulding.

6. As you make your mould and moulding, make notes on design sheet **5** about what happened.

1 The plastic sheet is clamped in place and then heated until it is soft.

2 A pump is then used to suck the air out from around the mould. This pulls the sheet down, forming the required shape.

3 Once cool the mould can be removed and used again to make another identical shape. The excess material is then trimmed away and the edge finished.

On your design sheet

- Say what might be difficult when making the mould and using the vacuum former. Explain what safety precautions you will take. **5**

Remember

- Vacuum forming can be used to make identical simple shapes, that have sloping sides.

The lid of the box for your game can be made from acrylic or manufactured board. You can finish this so it promotes your chosen star or company.

When you have designed and made all the parts of your game, you will need to assemble it.

Fasteners: permanent / non-permanent

There is a wide range of fasteners available. They include nails, screws, rivets, nuts and bolts.

Rivets are a **permanent** form of fixing as these can only be removed by drilling them out. **Non-permanent** fasteners can be removed and the parts reassembled at any time.

Screws have different shapes of head: **counter-sunk** or **round head**.

The head has either a **slot** or a Phillips **cross-shaped** recess in it that fits with the screwdriver.

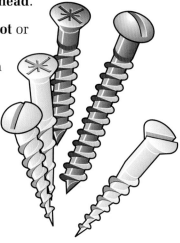

You will need to use screws to hold the top of your game in place. These can be easily removed if you wish to take your game apart. The four holes in the top need to be counter-sunk so the head of the screw does not stick up.

Instead of using counter-sinking for the top of the game, you could use a cup washer or a round-headed screw. However these could get caught when you put the game in a bag or pocket.

● On task 1 Work with materials

1. Cut the top of the box from a piece of acrylic or thin manufactured board.

2. Make the top the same size as the base of your game. Mark out the position of two holes, one at the start and another at the finish of your maze. Mark out the position of four other holes. These will be for the screws that will hold it in place.

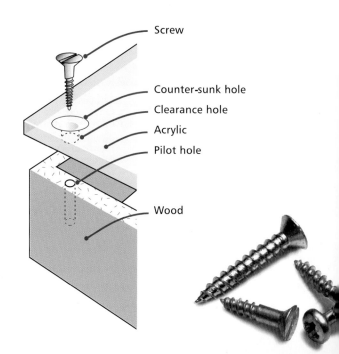

Screw

Counter-sunk hole

Clearance hole

Acrylic

Pilot hole

Wood

A sign of the times

Some scanners will cut thin vinyl that can then be stuck to your game. This is how many signs are now made and is called CAD/CAM: **computer-aided design/computer-aided manufacture**

By using a template or computer you can reproduce your logo as many times as you like.

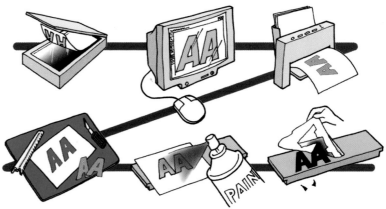

● **On task 2 Develop your design**

On design sheet **6a** design a silhouette of the logo or image that represents your star or organisation. Use this to make a template, so it can be used to finish the top. Ask your teacher if you can use a computer to help do this.

● **On task 3 Work with materials**

1. When all aspects of your design for your maze game have been sorted out, assemble the pieces and join them all together.

2. On design sheet **6b** explain how you decided to join the parts of your game. How did you overcome any problems you had while assembling the box?

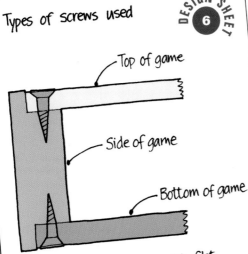

Types of screws used

DESIGN SHEET 6

Top of game

Side of game

Bottom of game

I decided to use screws with flat heads so they would fit into the countersunk holes. The countersunk holes keep the screws out of the way and stops them catching on things when you put the game away.

On your design sheets

- Describe how you designed and made the logo or image for your game. **6a**

- Explain how you assembled your game, and how you overcame any difficulties. **6b**

Remember

- There are two types of fasteners: permanent and non-permanent.

- Screws have different types of head.

Are You Receiving Me?

Good ideas are worthless unless they can be communicated to, and understood by, other people.

The next stage is to prepare a series of drawings that would enable someone else to manufacture your product.

Orthographic drawings

The arrangement of orthographic drawings and method of dimensioning them are defined by the British Standard No. 308. These are shown in a book (PD7308). The standard provides a common method for everyone to follow.

Remember that the correct arrangement of the drawings is very important (see pages 32–33).

When doing workshop drawings, neatness and accuracy are essential. Make sure you use a sharp pencil, a ruler and a set square or T-square, together with a drawing board.

You will need to choose a suitable scale.

▷ 1:1 means full size
▷ 1:2 means half size.

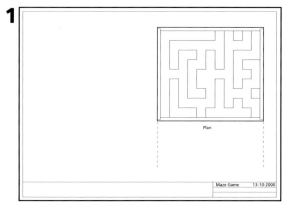

Draw plan and project lines down.

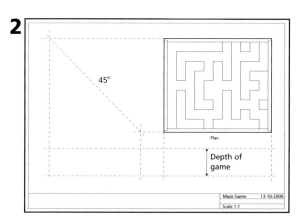

Project lines to show depth of game and add 45° line. Project lines for side view.

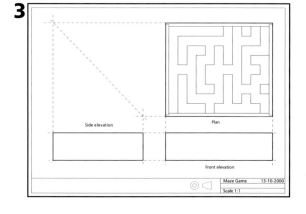

Draw in outlines of 3 views and add dimensions and details.

Putting on the dimensions

There are some general rules you need to follow when adding dimension lines to a drawing.

▷ All dimensions should be in millimetres.

▷ Numbers should be placed at the middle of the dimension line.

▷ Dimension and projection lines should be drawn lighter than the object (about half the thickness).

▷ Arrowheads should be triangular and filled in.

Some drawings use variations of these rules. The important thing is to ensure that whatever rules are used, they are applied consistently throughout the drawing.

Computer-aided design (CAD)

Many working drawings are now completed on a computer using CAD software. Drawings produced this way are more accurate and it is easy to make changes.

Many companies send their CAD drawings by electronic mail to factories around the world.

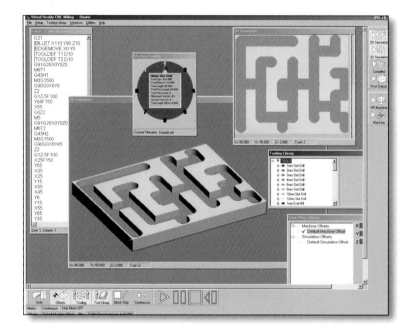

● On task Develop your design

Draw up your orthographic drawing on design sheet **7**. Make sure you plan it out first.

On your design sheet

● Complete your orthographic drawing. Remember to add dimensions. **7**

Remember

● Your final idea needs to be produced as a conventional orthographic drawing.

● Computer-aided design (CAD) will produce more accurate drawings, which are quicker and easy to change.

Now in 3D

A 3D (three-dimensional) drawing can be used to show what a product would look like. Colours, textures and shadow can help make it more realistic.

Going round in circles

Circles drawn in isometric are **ellipses**. Sets of **French Curves**, a drawing template, have isometric ellipses on them. Another way to draw ellipses is to *crate* them first (see page 33). Then you draw the circle inside.

It's not easy getting the circle looking right – it takes a lot of practice!

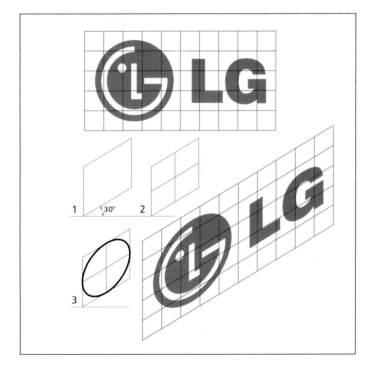

Producing a coloured rendering

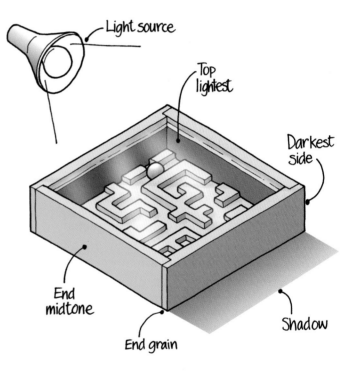

Light source

Top lightest

Darkest side

Shadow

End grain

End midtone

● On task 1 Apply what you know

Practise drawing isometric curves on design sheet **8a**. Draw some freehand, using grid paper. Make them into objects. Keep it simple at first!

● On task 2 Develop your design

1. Prepare a final isometric drawing of your game design. Ask your teacher to photocopy it. You can now use these copies to add colour, texture and shadow to your design. If you make a mistake you have not spoilt your original.

2. Put your product under a strong light, such as a spot lamp. This will show you which areas are light, mid-toned or dark and where the shadows are.

Exploding your idea

Exploded drawings are often used in instructions to show how something is put together. Look in the instruction manual for a product you have at home.

Exploded drawings are normally drawn in isometric.

Using CAD

CAD (**computer-aided design**) programs are very useful for producing coloured 3D and exploded design drawings. They take a long time to prepare, but details can be changed very quickly without having to re-do the entire drawing.

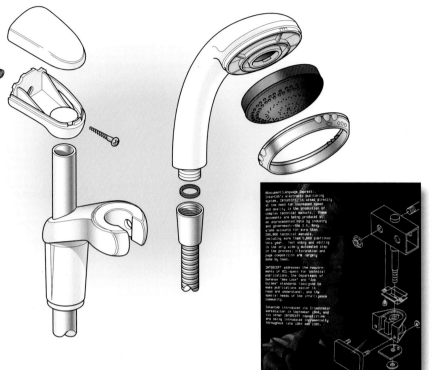

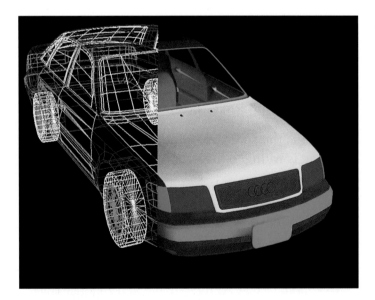

● On task 3 Develop your design

1. Find some examples of isometric and exploded drawings and diagrams in instruction leaflets from home.

2. On design sheet **8b** prepare an exploded drawing showing the different parts of your game.

Remember

- Use underlay grids and photocopies to help you produce quality drawings of your ideas.

- Use a bright light to model your work, to help you colour render your drawings.

- Exploded drawings are used to show how parts of a product are put together.

On your design sheets

- Draw a fully coloured isometric drawing of your design. **8a**

- Draw an exploded view of your maze game. **8b**

How Good is Your Game?

9

Amazing Mazes

Once you have finished making your game you will need to find out how successful your design is. You will need to carry out a variety of tests on it.

Meeting the requirements

The toy manufacturer wanted a design that:

▷ was based on the idea of a maze game
▷ would promote a famous person or organisation
▷ would fit in someone's pocket
▷ appealed to teenagers.

This was called the **design specification**

How well does your final design meet these requirements?

● *On task 1 Final evaluation*

Use sentences and drawings on design sheet **9a** to explain how well your final product meets the design specification.

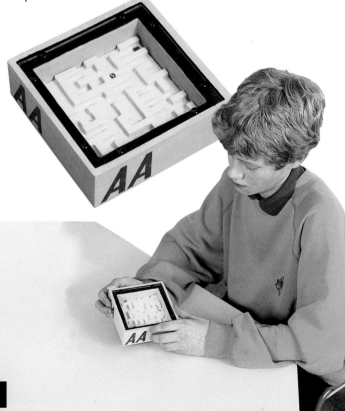

User tests

Give your maze game to a number of people to test it out. As well as your friends, this might include:

▷ parents

▷ a toy shop owner

▷ a fan of your chosen famous person.

Devise a series of questions for each person. For example:

▷ Was it easy to work out what the aim of the game was?

▷ How long did it take to solve?

▷ What is the company (or who is the person) the game is trying to promote?

▷ What suggestions have you got for improvements?

● *On task 2 Final evaluation*

1. Ask other people what they think of your game. Ask them to play with the game and suggest any improvements. Write these improvements on your design sheet **9a**.

2. Write out all the suggestions you have had from people, both the positive and negative. Are there some things that several people have said?

3. On design sheet **9b** produce some drawings showing how you could use these suggestions to improve your idea.

Mass production

In industry many plastic products are made using a process called **injection moulding**. Thermoplastic granules are heated up into a fluid state. They are then injected into a metal mould where they cool and harden.

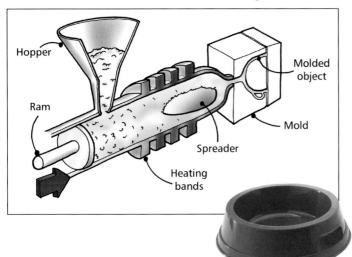

- Hopper
- Ram
- Spreader
- Heating bands
- Molded object
- Mold

● On task 3 Develop your design

1. Look at the 'Interview with... LEGO', on page 64–65, to learn more about the injection moulding process.

2. Find an old plastic toy, or some other product, that you can take apart. Study the moulded parts and see how they have been designed to fit together.

FORMULA FIGHTER

3. On design sheet **9c** show what ideas you have for redesigning your maze game to make it suitable for injection moulding.

You will probably need at least three different pieces. Show how these could be fitted together.

- ▶ What colours will you use?
- ▶ How could the promotional logo be included in the moulding?

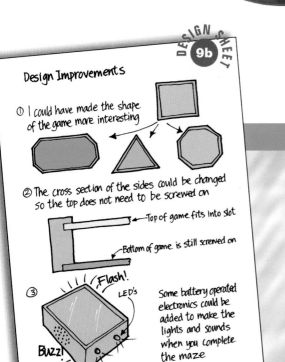

DESIGN SHEET 9b

Design Improvements

① I could have made the shape of the game more interesting

② The cross section of the sides could be changed so the top does not need to be screwed on

- Top of game fits into slot
- Bottom of game is still screwed on

③ Some battery operated electronics could be added to make the lights and sounds when you complete the maze

Flash! LED's
Buzz! Beep!

On your design sheets

- Discuss how well your design matches the specification. **9a**
- Record what other people said about your game. **9a**
- Make suggestions for design improvements. **9b**
- Suggest how the game could be designed to be suitable for injection moulding. **9c**

Remember

- Ask different people what they think of your design.
- Develop your design to make it more appealing to the target market, and to make it quicker and cheaper to manufacture.

An interview with...

LEGO bricks were invented by a Danish wooden toy company in 1947. They are now one of the world's most popular toys. But do you know how they are made?

Did you know that the word LEGO is a contraction of LEg GOdit, which in Danish means 'play well'?

How do LEGO bricks work? What are they made from?

“ The unique design of the current basic LEGO brick was patented in 1958 when an inner tube was added. This made the coupling of the bricks much stronger in construction, though they could still be easily pulled apart.

LEGO bricks are injection-moulded. A thermoplastic called ABS is used. This gives bright, shiny colours, maintains its shape well as it is resistant to scratching. The plastic granules are melted at approximately 235°C and are moulded under pressure. They harden and cool in the cold mould.

The production process is highly automated. Robots collect the finished LEGO pieces when a defined quantity have been moulded. The full boxes are given a special bar-code giving details of their contents. They are then collected by a robot truck and sent to the warehouse.

Red, blue, yellow, white, grey and black plastic granules are fed into the injection moulding machines.

The moulds are accurate to a tolerance of 0.005mm.

The various factory departments in which the products are assembled order the pieces when they are needed from the warehouse. Everything is controlled electronically. Staff only intervene if something goes wrong.

Specially designed machines are used for adding decoration such as faces, fitting arms and legs on figures or wheels on cars

Product testing is an important part of the process. The company philosophy is that 'only the best is good enough'.

The final stage of the production process involves packaging. Further machines help ensure that each LEGO set contains exactly the right number and type of pieces. "

What does the future hold for LEGO?

" Originally the LEGO company used to make wooden toys. Then it took advantage of new plastics technologies to expand its business. Now it's in the process of developing 'virtual' LEGO systems that take advantage of new information and communication technologies.

There is a LEGO web site (www.LEGO.com) which is well worth a visit. From here you can learn about the new electronic LEGO products which include the LEGO MINDSTORMS Robotics Invention System. "

Starting Point

Many millennia ago, dinosaurs ruled the world.
Now they're back!

Can you help DINO's DINER design a
menu for a new chain of themed cafés?

DINO's DINER is a new chain of high street cafés.
They are aimed at families and teenage children.
They specialise in doughnuts, ice-creams, cakes and
pastries, milk-shakes – all very unhealthy unless
part of a properly balanced diet, but undeniably fun
and profitable.

To make them highly distinctive they want their
outlets to be themed in the style of dinosaurs and
the *Modern Stone Age*. This theme is to be reflected
mainly through menus, furniture and fittings.

DINO's DINER have asked you to present them with
a series of designs for:

▷ a 3D pop-up menu, including a new DINO's
DINER logo

and a selection of the following:

▷ the interior of the cafés

▷ stone age furniture and
fittings

▷ other items of promotional
merchandising, e.g. badges,
key-rings, hats, etc.

▷ a web site.

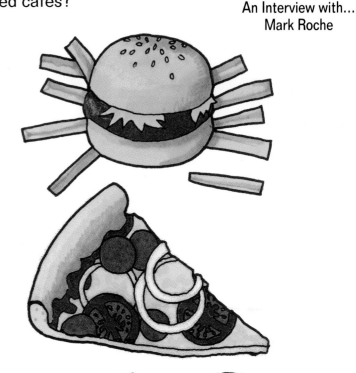

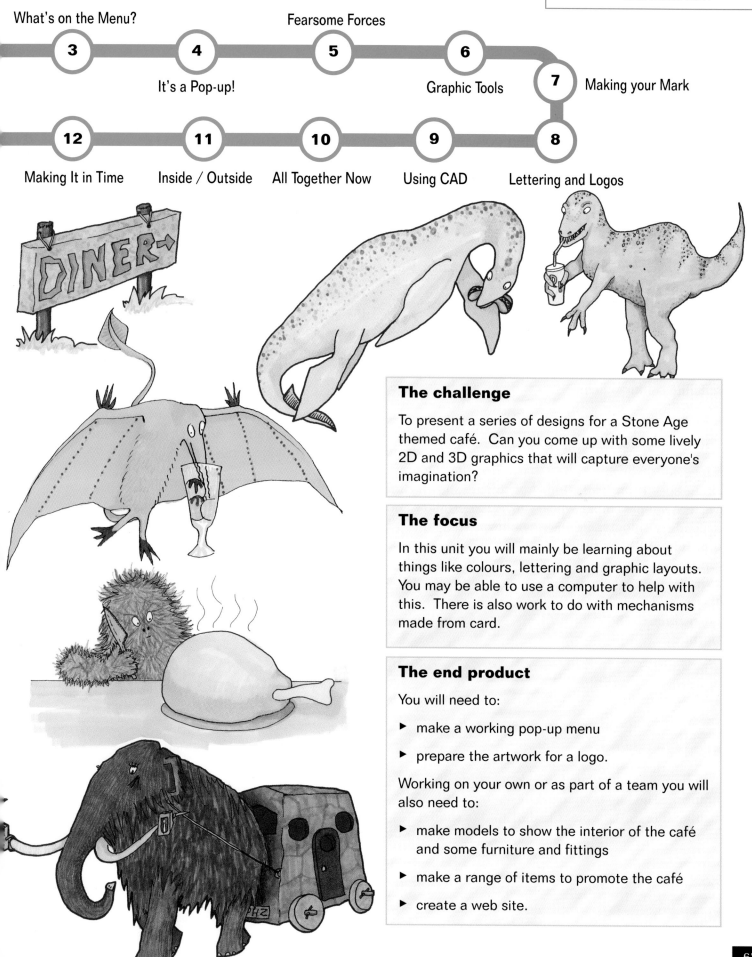

What's on the Menu?

3

4

Fearsome Forces

5

6

It's a Pop-up!

Graphic Tools

7 Making your Mark

12

11

10

9

8

Making It in Time

Inside / Outside

All Together Now

Using CAD

Lettering and Logos

The challenge

To present a series of designs for a Stone Age themed café. Can you come up with some lively 2D and 3D graphics that will capture everyone's imagination?

The focus

In this unit you will mainly be learning about things like colours, lettering and graphic layouts. You may be able to use a computer to help with this. There is also work to do with mechanisms made from card.

The end product

You will need to:

▶ make a working pop-up menu

▶ prepare the artwork for a logo.

Working on your own or as part of a team you will also need to:

▶ make models to show the interior of the café and some furniture and fittings

▶ make a range of items to promote the café

▶ create a web site.

Now in Colour

Colour is an essential ingredient in any design. You need to know something about harmonious and contrasting colours. You will also need to consider how different colours makes us feel and behave.

Colour plays an important part in the decisions we make about what to eat, and where to eat. It's not just the colour of the food that makes a difference but the colour of the surroundings.

Some colours seem to go well together. Others are good at providing contrast. How can you work out a suitable **colour scheme**?

The colour wheel

The colour wheel is a chart that shows the colours of the spectrum. The number of colours shown can vary. A simple colour wheel shows the **primary** and **secondary** colours. Primary colours are red, blue and yellow. When primary colours are mixed together they produce the secondary colours: green, orange and purple.

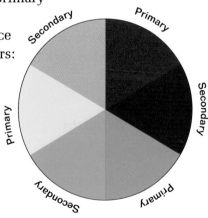

A colour is called a **hue** (for example blue or orange). The hue is changed by adding white to lighten it (a **tint**), or black to darken it (a **shade**).

100%　　　　　　　　　　　　　　0%

Complementary colours

Complementary colours are opposite each other on the colour wheel. They create **contrast** and make each colour look more intense. The colours next to each other on the colour wheel are in **harmony** with each other.

Remember that too many colours can look fussy. Keep your **colour scheme** simple. Use similar, harmonious colours. Add just one complementary colour to provide some contrast.

Which colour of computer would you choose?

Feeling blue?

Colours can be **symbolic**. That is they can mean something. What colour do you think is symbolic of the words *danger* and *stop*? What about *go, sunshine* and *evil*? Not all cultures have the same colour symbols. For example in China, white is linked with death and mourning.

● On task 1 Investigate

1. On design sheet **1a** create a patch of each primary and secondary colour and write notes saying what you associate with each of them.

2. Compare these with a partner's ideas. Do you agree or disagree?

Using colour

You will need to think about the colours that you use for your designs. This is important as it will help to create the image of the café.

What sort of colours might be appropriate for the *Modern Stone Age*?

▷ Is the food *simple* or *complicated*?
▷ Is the atmosphere *quiet* and *calm*, or *fun*?
▷ Are the staff *friendly* or *formal*?

Which colours could be linked to the words in italic?

● On task 2 Have good ideas

On design sheet **1b**, try out your ideas for suitable colours. Say if they are harmonious. Which colours provide some contrast? Are there too few or too many colours in your scheme? Do they help create the mood you want?

Remember

- The primary colours are red, blue and yellow.

- The secondary colours are orange, green and purple.

- A hue is a colour. A shade is a hue with black added. A tint is a hue with white added.

- Colours help to create image and atmosphere, and make us think of certain things.

- Don't use too many colours.

Colour association

DESIGN SHEET 1a

Primary colours

Red

Blue

Yellow

Heat, danger stop, football teams, racing cars, fire, Mars, Summer.

Cold, ice, the sea, the sky, football teams, Winter, sad.

Warm, spring-time, flowers, birds, gold, caution, happy, nice.

Secondary colours

Green

Orange

Flowers, chocolate, magic, Winter, sunset, sad.

Go, safe, trees, grass, the jungle, frogs, cool, restful.

Warm, fruit, the sun, comfort, happy, Autumn.

On your design sheets

- Show what you associate with different colours. **1a**

- Explain what colours you will be using and why. **1b**

Getting in the Mood

2

Creating a mood board will help you find lots of visual reference material for your final designs.

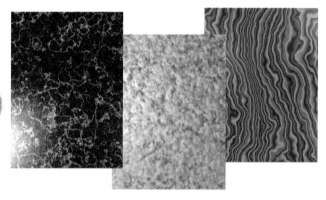

Images

Images are pictures that represent your design theme. Think about things like:

▷ dinosaurs

▷ rocks

▷ animal skins

▷ simple tools

▷ imaginary creatures.

Patterns and textures

Patterns and textures are also important in creating the right atmosphere. Which patterns and textures would be right for *Modern Stone Age*?

Lettering

Letters of the alphabet can come in many different shapes, sizes and colours. They can be plain or fancy, thick or thin, short or tall. There is more about styles of lettering, or **typography** on page 82.

What sorts of letters might be suitable for DINO's DINER?

Mood board

A **mood board** is a way of displaying colours, shapes, patterns and images together that produces the mood that you are aiming for.

Mood boards are also useful for seeing how tints and shades of different colours work, or do not work, together.

Putting a mood board together requires some thought, experimentation and planning. First you need to assemble all the images, colours, patterns and textures. Then try different arrangements of them on the paper or board you are working on.

Here are some guidelines for composing a mood board:

▷ work outwards from the centre

▷ avoid leaving large areas of white, or any other background colour, near the centre

▷ make sure there is a good balance of images and colours across the board

▷ try overlapping images and words, so they all link together visually.

● *On task 1 Investigate*

Look through magazines, books and on the Internet to find examples of the sorts of images, patterns, textures and styles of lettering suggested on the page opposite.

► Cut out, trace and draw images that appeal to you.

► Add samples of lettering.

► Use the ideas for colours that you recorded on design sheet **1a**.

● *On task 2 Have good ideas*

Plan your mood board. When you think you've got it right, carefully fix all the things down onto design sheet **2**.

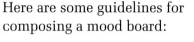

● Create your mood board. **2**

> **Remember**
>
> ● A mood board includes examples of images, colours, patterns, textures and lettering that will be used in a design.

What's on the Menu?

3

Looking at the design of some existing themed menus will give you some ideas about what you might be able to do.

SUNDAE'S
Stands up on table when folded

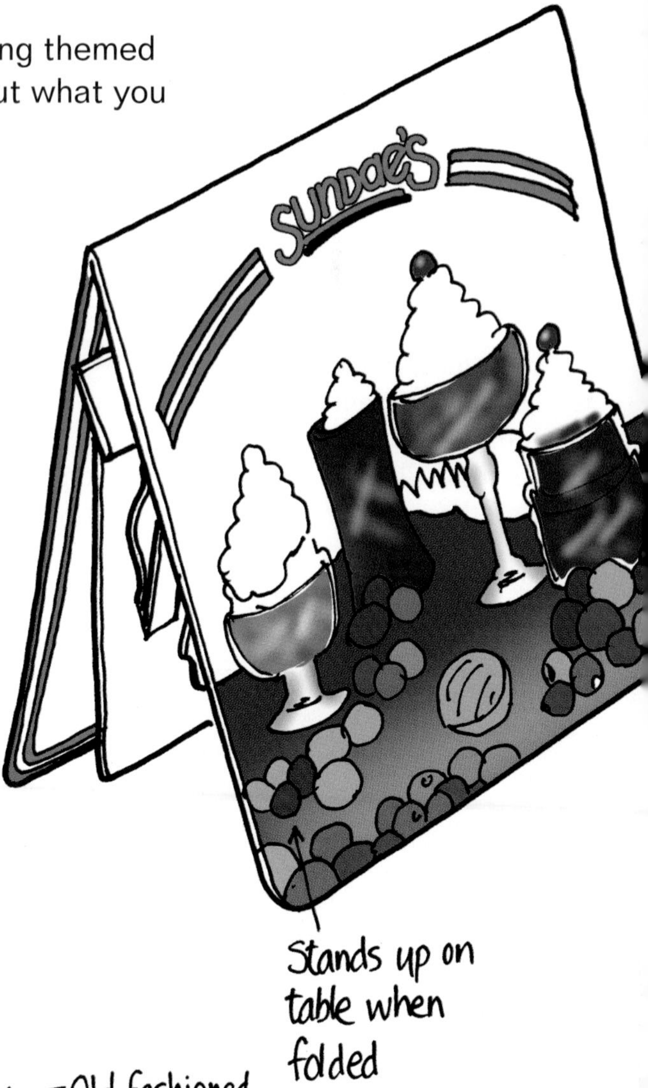

You will need some themed restaurant menus. It does not matter if they are not aimed at families or children.

● *On task Evaluate*

1. Working in your group, discuss the following questions:

- What colour schemes have been used?
- What patterns and textures have been used?
- What styles of lettering have been used (see page 82)?

In your discussion try to use some of the following words: bright, subtle, imaginative, cheerful, sophisticated, smart, fun, elegant, bold, dull.

Also try to compare the different menus. For example: 'The lettering in this menu is colourful and easy to read, whereas in this one it's too fussy and almost illegible.'

Finally discuss which you think is the best designed menu and say why.

2. On design sheet **3** sketch one or more of the menus and add notes to describe and evaluate each one.

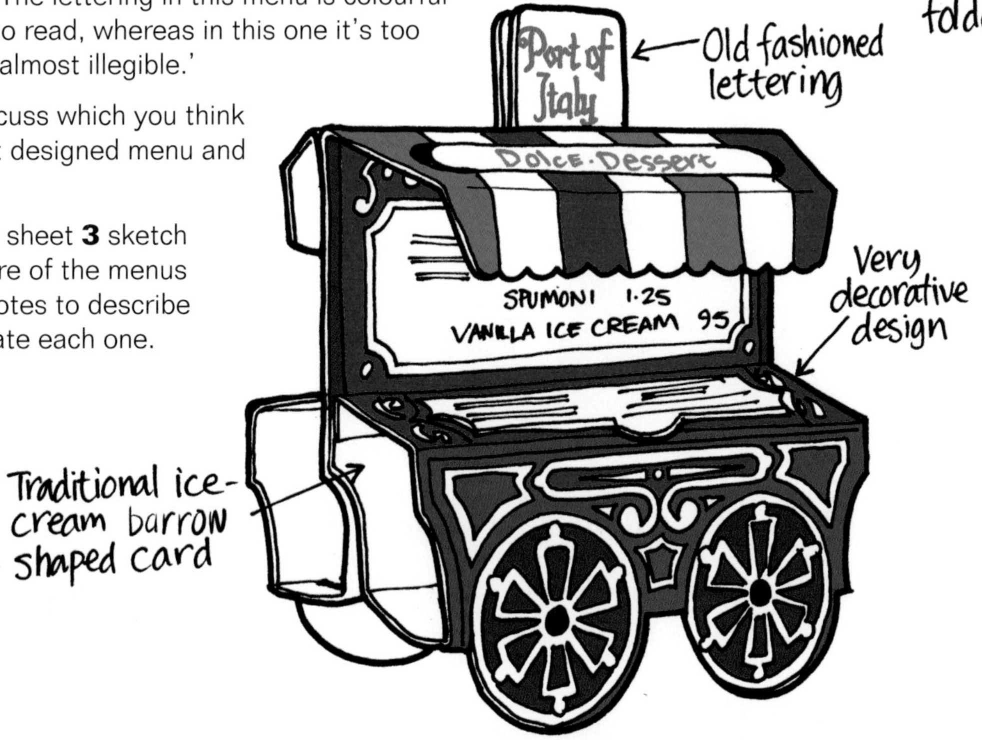

Port of Italy
Old fashioned lettering
Dolce . Dessert
SPUMONI 1.25
VANILLA ICE CREAM 95
Very decorative design
Traditional ice-cream barrow shaped card

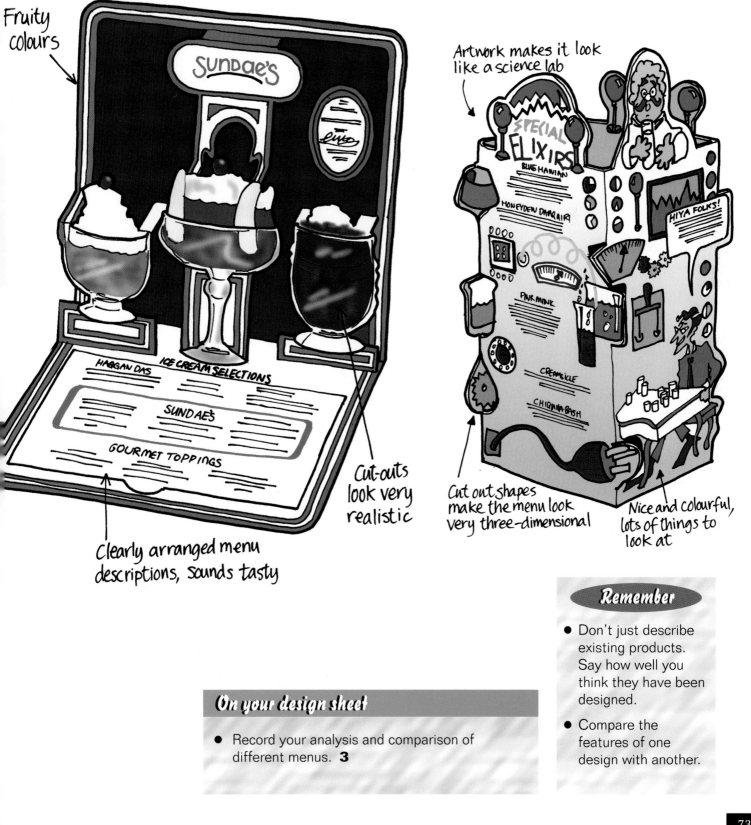

Fruity colours

Sundae's

ICE CREAM SELECTIONS

HAGGAN DAS

SUNDAE'S

GOURMET TOPPINGS

Clearly arranged menu descriptions, sounds tasty

Cut-outs look very realistic

Artwork makes it look like a science lab

SPECIAL ELIXIRS

BLUE HAWIAN

HONEYDEW DAIQAIRI

HIYA FOLKS!

PINK MINK

CREAMSICLE

CHIQANA BASH

Cut out shapes make the menu look very three-dimensional

Nice and colourful, lots of things to look at

Remember

- Don't just describe existing products. Say how well you think they have been designed.

- Compare the features of one design with another.

On your design sheet

- Record your analysis and comparison of different menus. **3**

It's a Pop-up!

A pop-up mechanism will make your menu stand out.

The DINO's DINER menu

You have been asked to design a special promotional menu for DINO's DINER. The menu should attract attention and describe two different special items the cafe sells.

To be successful it must:

▷ be 3D in some way and contain a pop-up mechanism

▷ be visually based on the *Modern Stone Age* theme

▷ be no bigger than 200 mm in any direction when closed

▷ be durable and easily wiped clean.

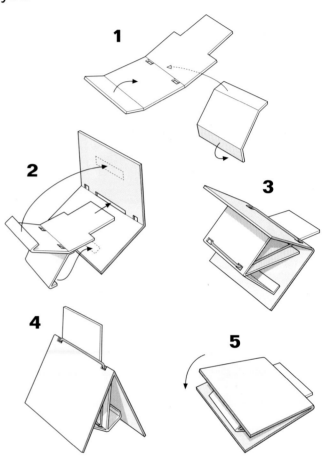

Pop-up triangle

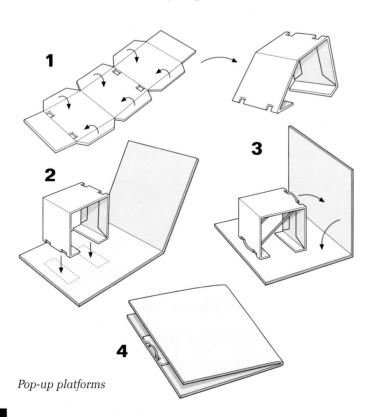

Pop-up platforms

Animated attention

Colour and a strong image can grab attention. **Movement** is another good way of gaining our interest.

You may have made simple pop-ups with folds and hinges in the past. This time you will be using an elastic band to produce the 'pop-up' effect.

To help you, there are some examples of these mechanisms shown above. You do not have to use them. You may want to choose one that has the effect you want or adapt one to suit your needs.

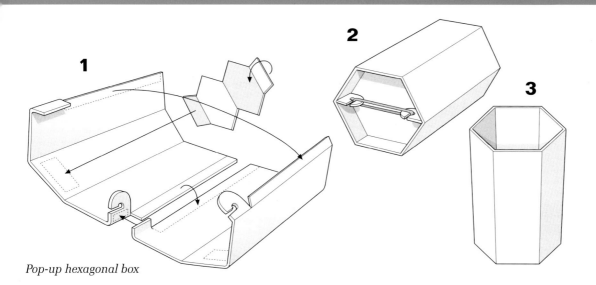

Pop-up hexagonal box

● On task 1 Have good ideas

1. Look back at your *Modern Stone Age* mood board. Which images, colours, textures, etc. might be suitable for your menu? Think carefully about how you might use the pop-ups shown, or your own ideas, to make your menu move.

2. On design sheet **4a** make notes and sketches of your ideas for a pop-up menu. Make some quick and simple experimental models. Describe and evaluate them. Explain how they will work. What does the elastic band do?

● On task 2 Develop your design

1. Decide which pop-up mechanism you will use. Say why on design sheet **4b**.

2. Make a full-size working model of it to check it works.

3. Look carefully to see where there may be problems and try to solve these. For example some areas may need strengthening. Explain what happened on design sheet **4b**.

On your design sheets

- Make notes and sketches about how you might use a pop-up mechanism to animate your ideas. **4a**

- Decide which mechanism will give you the effect that you want. Make notes and sketches about this. **4b**

- Make notes about where there may be problems. How did you try to solve them? **4b**

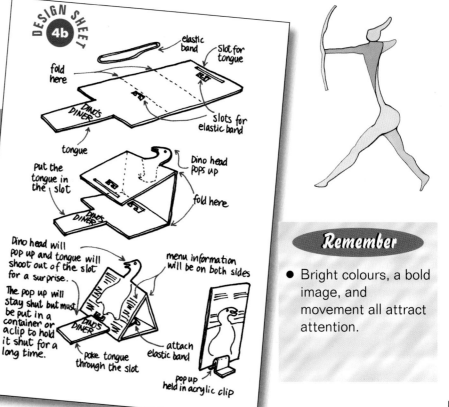

Remember

- Bright colours, a bold image, and movement all attract attention.

Fearsome Forces

5

All structures have forces acting on them, including your 3D pop-up menu! After you've studied the following you should be able to explain how your 3D pop-up menu works.

The different sorts of structures were discussed on pages 34–35. Not all **forces** are the same. Here are five types: compression, tension, shear, torsion or twist and bending. You may know of others.

The foot is squashing the drinks can. The force the foot is putting on the can is **compression**.

The dinos are too heavy for the see-saw, they are bending it. The force on the beam of the see-saw is **bending**.

The pencil is being twisted in the sharpener. The force on the pencil is **torsion**.

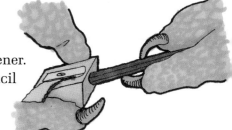

The two dinos having a tug of war are pulling the rope. The force on the rope is **tension**.

Each of the scissor blades is putting an opposite force on the hair, the result is a hair cut! The force on the hair is **shear**.

Internal Force / External Force

On balance

When the internal and external forces acting on a structure balance each other out, we say that a structure is in **equilibrium** or **balance**. This means it does not break or fail.

You will need to make sure that your menu is in equilibrium. This means the forces acting on it do not cause it to break or fail.

On task Apply what you know

1. On design sheet **5a** draw a different example of each of the types of force shown above and label it with the correct name.

2. What types of forces are acting on your pop-up menu? Draw a diagram on design sheet **5b** to illustrate this.

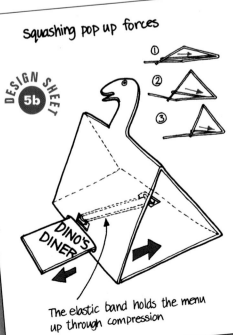

squashing pop up forces

DESIGN SHEET **5b**

① ② ③

DINO'S DINER

The elastic band holds the menu up through compression

On your design sheets

- Draw five different examples of forces and label them. **5a**

- Draw a diagram to illustrate the forces on your pop-up. **5b**

Remember

- There are several different types of forces.

- Forces have to be balanced so that a structure stays in equilibrium.

Graphic Tools

6

Cutting and colouring paper and card needs just as much care and accuracy as when using other materials.

When you make your pop-up menu you will have to aim for a professional finish. This means that you will have to use tools and equipment very carefully so that all of the cuts are clean, the folds are crisp and the finishes are perfect.

You will need to work on a clean, flat surface.

On the mat

The best surface to cut on is a cutting mat. It is able to *self heal* when you cut into it. It has grids on it to help you to line up your work. It also stops your scalpel or knife from getting blunt as quickly as it would on a hard surface. The surface is slightly non-slip which helps you to control the card you are cutting.

The correct term for card of all thicknesses is *board*.

At the cutting edge

The scalpel is the best tool for making cuts which are either curved or do not start and finish at the edge of the paper. This is a fine blade attached to a handle. It is very sharp and great care must be taken when using it.

An alternative often found in schools is the Stanley knife. As long as this has a sharp blade it is a very good substitute.

Remember that you are more likely to be cut by a blunt blade than a sharp one. This is because you do not need to struggle to cut with a sharp blade.

If your blade is not very sharp or the board you are using is thick, cut along the same line several times until you cut through it.

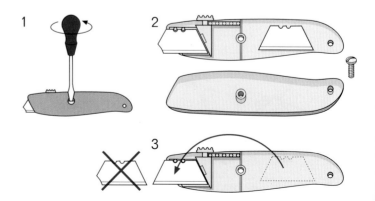

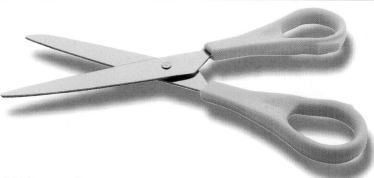

Following the rules

▷ If you are cutting straight lines, you must use a safety ruler. This is a ruler with a valley running down its length which protects your fingers from the blade of a knife or scalpel. Be warned that safety rulers often have a couple of millimetres before the start of the scale. This can lead to confusion when measuring.

▷ If you are cutting curved lines, always use your fore finger and thumb to make a bridge and cut between them. Never cut towards your fingers, keep them well out of the way.

Using scissors

▷ When you use scissors, make sure that you do not finish the cut at the end of the blades or you will end up with a little tear at the end. Try to finish the cut about 1 cm before the end of the blade.

▷ Just like scalpels and knives, blunt scissors are dangerous.

▷ If you use scissors to crease a fold, be careful how you hold them. Do not wrap your fingers around the blades. Make the first pass with the scissors quite light and follow this with a firmer stroke. Do not press down too hard or you will crumple up the surface of the board.

● On task Work with materials

On design sheet **6** write two safety tips for each of these tools:

► a cutting mat
► a scalpel or knife
► a safety ruler
► a pair of scissors.

On your design sheet

● Say what safety rules you would follow when using a number of graphic tools.

Remember

● You need to create a professional finish when you make your menu.

● Make sure you use the right tools in the right way.

Making your Mark

7

There are many different sorts of media and materials you can use when creating a graphic product.

Pencils

Graphite pencils come in a range of hardnesses. For example a 2H pencil will give you a precise line, and stay sharper. A 2B pencil is much softer, and is better for quick sketching and adding tone.

An HB comes in the middle of the range and is a good all-purpose pencil.

Coloured pencils

Coloured pencils provide a soft, textured surface. They can be overlaid to produce tones and tints.

Chalks and pastels

Chalks and pencils are an alternative to coloured pencils and felt pens. They can be very effective at showing 3D form and textured surfaces, particularly on top of coloured papers.

Felt markers

These come in a wide range of shapes, sizes and colours. Choose a thickness according to how large an area you want to cover. Aim to use neat, even strokes, rather than 'scribbling' with it.

Try the pen out on a piece of scrap paper or card first to see what the results are like, and to check the ink does not go through the paper too far.

Technical pens

There are also many sorts of fine-line black and coloured ink pens that can be used for very neat accurate work. They often come in specific nib widths (e.g. 0.5 mm). Some can be refilled.

Papers and boards

There are hundreds of different types of paper and board to choose from. They vary in colour, texture and thickness (called 'weight').

Get to know the different sorts that are available in school. Look in an art supplies shop for a range of more unusual papers.

Mixed media

In most cases you will need to use more than one mark-making device when preparing a graphic product. Try combining graphite pencils with felt pens. Add a fine line drawn with a technical pen to the outline of a pencil drawing.

Think about the materials you are trying to represent. A rough wooden surface will probably look more convincing when coloured pencils are used. A smooth plastic or metal surface will probably be better with a large area of flat colour applied with a felt pen.

At the finish

The surface of a graphic can easily get damaged. It needs to be protected as much as possible.

If you've been using chalks or pastels they need to be sprayed with a fixative. Other sorts of media can be protected with a sheet of adhesive transparent vinyl. Your school may have a special machine for doing this.

If you've been working on paper, you might want to mount your work on card.

Getting into print

Most graphic products are printed in quantity. There are lots of different ways of creating a printed surface. Which method is used depends on the number required and the quality of print needed.

If you wanted to print up a small number of T-shirts, the best method would probably be **screen printing**. At the other end of the scale a daily newspaper uses a process called **lithography**.

In school there are only limited options. A **photocopier** is one method, though probably restricted to black and white. Another possibility is to use a computer printer. Make sure you check out the cost of paper and inks first!

● On task Investigate

1. Experiment with as wide a range of media as possible. Do this on design sheet **7**. Note down which media you used, and add some comments about how easy or difficult each is, and what it might be used for.

2. Find out what printing or finishing methods you might be able to use. Note down what you discover on design sheet **7**.

Media Experimentation

DESIGN SHEET 7

Wax crayon
Don't like this

Felt tip pen
Good for drawing with but not easy to use.

Marker pens
Good for colouring large areas

Pencil crayon
A good range of colours. How hard you press makes a big difference.

Graphic Pen

Edding graphic painters
Too difficult to use!

Ready mix paints

Painting

Printing

On your design sheet

● Record your experiments with a range of graphic media. **7**

Remember

● Decide what effect you are trying to create and choose the best media.

● Work with care and accuracy.

Lettering and Logos

8

The design and application of different styles of lettering is called typography.

Most companies have their own logo or symbol to identify them. To design a logo you will need to know something about typography.

36 Delicious Flavours

Typography

Choosing the style

There are thousands of different styles of lettering. The different styles are known as **fonts**. Some are **plain** and easy to read in long lines. One of the most popular is called:

Times Roman

Many books and magazines use this **traditional** typeface, or a variation of it. A popular **modern** design is called:

Helvetica

This is sometimes used for long columns of text, but more often for headings or titles. Again there are a number of variations that can be used.

Other styles are described as being **decorative**. These are useful for attracting attention. Here are a couple of examples:

HANDEL GOTHIC

Script

Decorative typefaces can be difficult to read. Therefore they should only be used for short headings or titles.

When choosing typefaces for a design it's a good idea not to use more than two different fonts.

Getting the size right

Choosing the size of lettering is very important. There are two things that need to be considered.

First, the **height** of a letter. This is measured in points. The text you are reading now is 11 pt, which is about 2.5 mm high. Text that is less than 10 pt can be difficult to read.

A subheading needs to be a little larger. These are usually around 14 pt. The main title on a page needs to be a lot larger. The one at the top of this page is 36 pt.

Second is the **thickness** of a letter. For example the same style can be:

Light   Condensed   **Bold**

▷ If you have a lot of space you want to fill, choose a large point size, and a light thickness.

▷ If you only have a small space to fill, choose a small point size, and a bold thickness.

Special effects

Letters can be in italic. Another possibility is outline. They can also include a shadow.

Italic

OUTLINE

Shadow

Designing logos and symbols

Logos and symbols make it easy to identify a particular company or organisation. A good design will also say something about the quality of the products and services it provides, for example, modern, reliable, friendly, etc.

Designs are usually based on one of the following:

▷ the initial letters of the company (e.g. BhS, M&S)

▷ the whole name of the company (e.g. Ford, ASDA, LEVI'S)

▷ an image of the product or service being sold (e.g. British Gas)

▷ an abstract pattern (e.g. The Body Shop).

Often a combination of these approaches is used.

An important key to success is simplicity!

● On task Investigate / Develop your design

1. Collect some old newspapers, magazines and packages. Cut out a variety of different types of logos and symbols. Fix them on design sheet **8a** and add labels to say what type, or combination of types, each is (e.g. initial letters and pattern).

2. Choose any two logos or symbols. On design sheet **8b** copy them out neatly. Make each one fill half the sheet. Use drawing instruments. Add colour. Try to match the colours as closely as possible. Can you identify whether plain, decorative, light, bold or italic typefaces have been used?

3. On design sheet **8c** develop your design ideas for a logo for DINO's DINER. Start by experimenting with different ideas. Then choose one approach and work on it in more detail. Make sure you choose your style of lettering carefully. Think in detail about the colours you use.

On your design sheets

● Make a collection of logos and symbols and say what type they are. **8a**

● Make a detailed, accurate copy of two of them. **8b**

● Develop ideas for a logo for DINO's DINER. **8c**

Remember

● There are lots of different styles and sizes of lettering to choose from.

● The best logos and symbols are usually the most simple ones.

Using CAD

9

ICT (information and communication technology) provides a quick and easy way to model ideas as well as producing excellent quality finished products.

Modelling

Modelling can be carried out using 2D and 3D **computer-aided design** packages (CAD). These help you to draw your ideas quickly and accurately on the computer screen.

Graphics packages have drawing and painting tools and a palette of colours. The images you make are easy to change. Because you do not have to spend time drawing ideas on paper, you can put more time into experimenting and getting the best possible result.

2D CAD drawing and painting tools

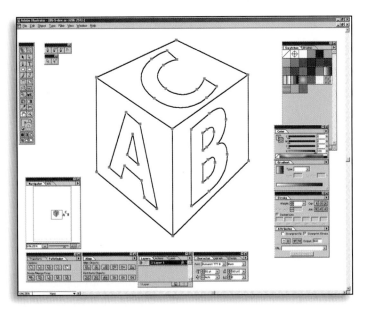

Bitmap and vector graphics

There are two sorts of graphics packages, bitmap and vector.

Bitmap packages store images by noting the position and colour of each dot of colour in the picture. Photographic images and Paint programs use bitmaps. It is easy to make overall changes to the whole image, e.g. make it lighter or darker. Different parts of the image can be selected, but this can be difficult to do accurately. The size of bitmap files can be very big.

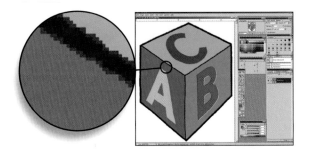

Vector packages store images by noting the length and angle of each line of the image. Drawing packages use vector graphics. It is easy to make detailed changes to lines and shapes and to move the different elements around. Most clip art images are created in vector packages.

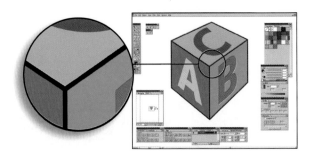

Ready-made images

Existing printed images or your own drawings can be scanned into the computer. Alternatively you can use **clip art**. This is a range of images which are ready-made graphics files.

You can find clip art on the Internet and on CD-ROMs. Some are free from copyright, others you have to buy or get a license to use. Be aware that some clip art images are of poor quality. You need to be selective in the type and number that you use.

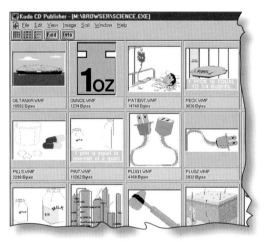

Ready-made photos

There are also CD-ROMs that provide photographs. Be warned that these may be too big to keep a copy of on a floppy disk.

Photographs can be scanned in directly. Software is available which will make changes to photographs. For example areas can be recoloured, parts of images removed and others redrawn.

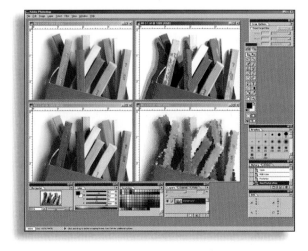

Text and image

Text can be added into a graphic file. Graphics can be pasted into a text document.

● On task Investigate

Check what ICT equipment is available for you to use. Not all of the packages described here may be available to you. You may be able to design on screen in colour, but not have access to a colour printer. Your school may not have a colour scanner.

Make notes on design sheet **9** on what facilities you have and how you might be able to use them in your project to design and make your menu.

On your design sheet

- Explain how you might be able to use ICT to help you design and make your graphic product. **9**

Remember

- Make sure you use the correct program to achieve the results you want.

All Together Now

10

Your next task is to design the layout of the final menu, including the list of food available and your graphics images.

Layout grids

Use a **layout grid** to make your work look professional. This is a framework that shows the spaces for the main areas of text and illustration.

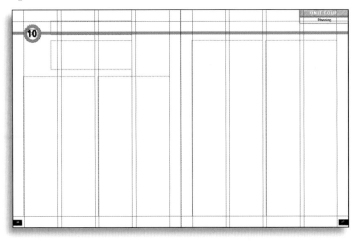

The framework is made from a series of vertical and horizontal lines. This shows the position of the margins, columns and headings.

Use a layout grid to help you decide where to place blocks of text and images so they look balanced on the page. The page that you are looking at has been based on a layout grid.

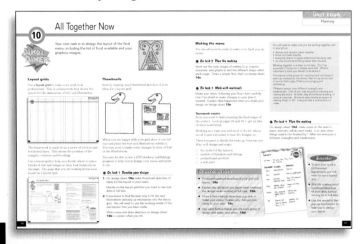

Thumbnails

Start by making small *thumbnail* sketches of your ideas for a layout grid.

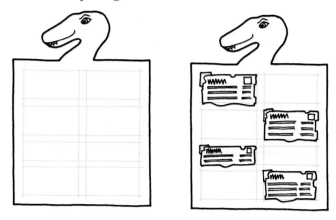

When you are happy with your grid draw it out full size and place the text and illustrations within it. You may need to make some changes in sizes of font or the illustrations.

You may be able to use a DTP (desktop publishing) program to help you to design your menu and print it out.

● *On task 1 Develop your design*

1. On design sheet **10a** make thumbnail sketches of ideas for the layout of your menu.

   Decide on the layout grid that you want to use and draw it full size.

2. Experiment to find the best way to fit the text, illustrations and pop-up mechanism into the layout grid. You will need to use the working model of the mechanism that you have made.

   Write notes and draw sketches on design sheet **10b** to explain what you did.

Making the menu

You should now be ready to make your final pop-up menu.

● On task 2 Plan the making

Work out the main stages of making (e.g. prepare materials, add graphics) and the different steps within each stage. Draw a simple flow-chart on design sheet **10c**.

● On task 3 Work with materials

Make your menu, following your flow-chart carefully. Don't be afraid to make changes to your plan if needed. Explain what happened when you made your design on design sheet **10c**.

Teamwork counts

Now you need to start planning the final stages of the project. Look at pages 88 and 89 to get an idea of what is involved.

Working as a team you will need to decide whose mood board and menu to base the designs on.

Then you need to divide the tasks up between you. Who will design and make:

▷ the model of the interior
▷ models of furniture and fittings
▷ promotional products
▷ a web site?

On your design sheets

- Produce thumbnail sketches of your grid and layout. **10a**

- Explain the decisions you made when finalising the design while working at full size. **10b**

- Draw a flow chart to show how you plan to make your menu. Explain any changes you made to your plan. **10c**

- Say what further things you are each going to design and make, and when. **10d**

You will need to make sure you are working together well in your group:

- discuss and develop ideas together
- share out tasks equally
- everyone needs to agree what should be done next
- no-one should be working harder than the rest.

Working together in a team is not easy. Don't be surprised if things don't always work well. What's important is what you decide to do about it.

If someone in the group isn't working hard, and doesn't seem as involved as the others, then it's up to the rest of you to find a way of being encouraging and motivating.

Different people have different strengths and weaknesses. One of you may be good at planning and making decisions. Another may be better at drawing, or using a computer. Someone else may be an expert at making things in 3D. Everyone has a contribution to make.

● On task 4 Plan the making

On design sheet **10d**, make notes on the team's plans, and who will do each task. Is it clear when things need to be finished by? What are everyone's different strengths and weaknesses?

DESIGN SHEET 10d

Teamwork

Our team: – Me, Gary, Paul, Amy, Hajra and Danielle

Team member	Strengths	Weaknesses
Gary	Ideas, Research	Drawing
Paul	Computers	Won't do anything else
Amy	Computers, Organising things	Bossy. Tells everyone what to do
Hajra	Drawing, Cutting-out, Computers	Argues with Amy a lot
Danielle	Ideas, Cutting-out, Making things in 3D	Drawing and Colouring
Me	Drawing and Colouring, Making things in 3D	Computers and Research

Remember

- To give your work a professional appearance you will need to use a layout grid.

- Start by making small *thumbnail* sketches of your ideas before moving on to full size.

- Use the model of the pop-up mechanism to help you to design your layout.

Inside / Outside

11

Which other designs are you going to include in your final presentation? DINO's DINER said they would be interested in seeing your ideas for things like the interior of the cafés, items of furniture and fittings, promotional products, and a web site.

On the inside

Each café will occupy a rectangular floor-size of about 10 metres wide by 20 metres deep. How could this space be divided up?

What materials, colours, patterns and textures will be used for the walls, flooring, curtains, paintwork, etc?

How could the *Modern Stone Age* theme be developed through a range of wall surfaces, chairs, tables, counters and cupboards?

Making it up

What materials could you use to make **models** of your interior, furniture and fittings?

Often you will need to use a different material to represent another. How might you use the following:

▷ dowel rods
▷ plastic straws
▷ modelling foam
▷ coloured/textured cards and papers
▷ papier maché
▷ wire.

Pay close attention to detail. It's often the details that make a model look realistic.

Spreading the word

Making sure people know about a new product or service is very important. There are so many new businesses trying to catch our attention, it's difficult to get noticed.

Companies use every opportunity to put their logo or symbol on items that customers may take away with them. What could DINO's DINER do?

On the Web

Can you design a web site for DINO's DINER? It could provide things like:

▷ details of where their cafés are
▷ examples of their menus
▷ a party delivery service
▷ a customer feed-back form.

Prepare a number of trial screens to show how the site might look. Draw a site map to show what might be on it.

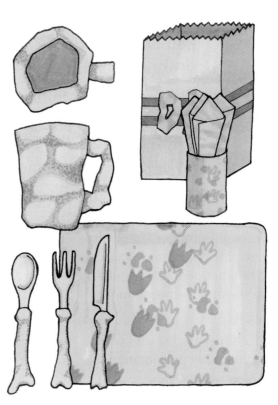

● **On task**
Develop your design / Plan the making

1. On design sheet **11a**, develop your designs for the interior of the café's furniture and fittings, promotional ideas and/or a web site you have. Use plenty of coloured sketches and notes to show and explain your ideas.

2. On design sheet **11b**, show how you plan to make what you have designed.

On your design sheets

● Show how you have developed your design ideas. **11a**

● Describe how you will make your design. **11b**

Remember

● Make a plan of work and check it carefully for possible mistakes before you begin making.

● Make notes of any changes that you make to your plan of work.

Showing Off

12

You need to prepare a presentation of your pop-up menu and the other items you have designed. Then you need to evaluate them.

Finally, you need to think about how well you tackled the process of designing and making.

Communication counts

It is not enough to have designed and made a successful product. Your ideas and plans need to be communicated effectively to other people who will be involved in making your designs a reality.

The final challange in this unit is to prepare a convincing presentation of your ideas.

● On task 1 Final evaluation

Work as a group and prepare a short presentation (no more than three minutes long) for the rest of your class to explain your ideas. Focus on the features of your designs, rather than how you developed your ideas. You will need to discuss and agree:

▶ What are the key points of the designs?

▶ Who is going to do the talking?

▶ What visual material will be shown?

▶ What comes first and what comes last?

Record your group's decisions and plans on design sheet **12a**.

Try to find time to rehearse the presentation. Make sure it does not last longer than three minutes.

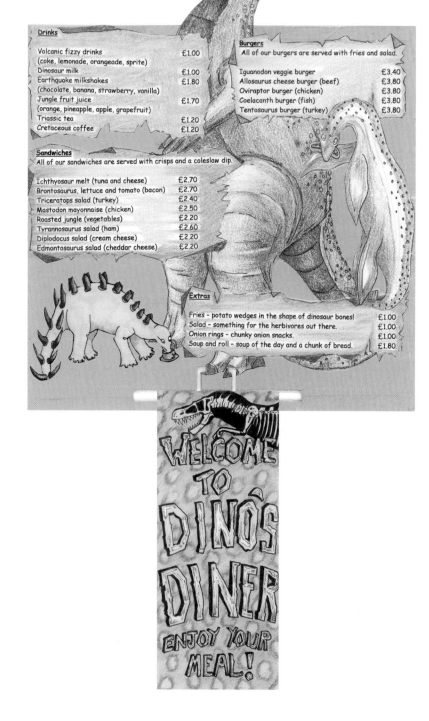

Evaluating the product, process and presentation

When you are evaluating the work you have done in this project you need to discuss:

▷ how successful the products were that you designed and made

▷ how well you worked

▷ how well you presented your ideas.

● On task 2 Final evaluation

1. In pairs, write down on design sheet **12b** all the things that your designs needed to do. Working together, decide how successful each of your designs has been for each of these criteria.

2. Give each one a score out of three. Three means that it has achieved it very well. One means that it has just managed to achieve it.

3. Give reasons for your decisions. For example, the menu may be based on the theme of the *Modern Stone Age*, but it doesn't make the name of the café very clear. Therefore it may only get a score of two.

● On task 3 Final evaluation

1. Choose two aspects of the way in which you worked (e.g. investigation, planning the making) that went well. On design sheet **12c** explain how you made progress in these aspects.

2. Choose two aspects of the way in which you worked (e.g. having good ideas, working with materials) that did not go as well as you would have liked. On design sheet **12c** explain how you might improve in these aspects of your work in your next project.

● On task 4 Final evaluation

How well did your final presentation go?

▶ Was everything ready on time?

▶ Did everyone remember what to say?

▶ Did the audience understand your design ideas?

Record your answers to these questions on design sheet **12d**.

On your design sheets

- Plan your group's final presentation. **12a**
- Evaluate your final products. **12b**
- Evaluate how well you worked. **12c**
- Evaluate your final presentation. **12d**

An Interview with...

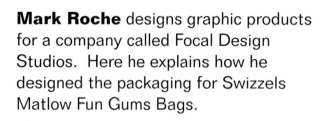

13

Mark Roche designs graphic products for a company called Focal Design Studios. Here he explains how he designed the packaging for Swizzels Matlow Fun Gums Bags.

Focal Design Studios Ltd

CREATIVE DESIGN
AND MARKETING
COMMUNICATIONS

Can you explain what your company does?

❝ Most of our work is about creating an image for a product and then packaging and advertising it. For example, Muller dairy yoghurts and Swizzels Matlow sweets, makers of Lovehearts and Drumstick lollies. ❞

How do you know what the client wants?

❝ The account manager gathers information from the client. Using this information, they write a design brief. This will include information about how much the client wants to spend and how much time we have to develop our ideas. There may be any initial ideas that they might have had, for example the use of a cartoon character.

From this brief, the designers come up with a range of ideas. These are presented to the client who decides which they want to develop further. ❞

What was the design brief for Swizzels Matlow Fun Gums Bags?

❝ The shapes for Swizzels Matlow 10p Fun Gums Bags of sweets already existed. Swizzels Matlow were aware that many local authorities were frowning on the sale of unwrapped sweets by confectionary retailers, e.g. loose jellies sold from plastic tubs. This was because of the risk of contamination. What we had to do was to develop a way of selling them in a hygienic way.

We knew the style that the company use for brightly coloured fun packaging that appeals to children. This is what we based our ideas on. So for the Fun Gums Bags it had to be hygienic, it had to be in line with the well known company image and it had to be cost effective. ❞

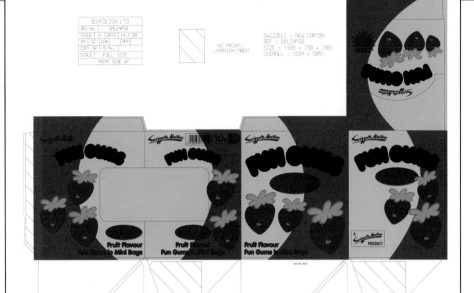

Where do your ideas come from?

" Using the 10p Swizzels Matlow Fun Gums Bags example again, we had to work within a number of design constraints.

The client had told us how many sweets needed to be in each bag, so this gave us an idea of the size.

We knew that the printing process they wanted to use could only handle a limited number of colours.

The colours needed to be bright and attractive and appeal to the target market, mainly children and young people.

The designer had to come up with ideas that took all of this into account. Designers all have different strengths and I am suited to drawing cartoons and designs which appeal to young people. Therefore I was chosen to work on the Swizzels Matlow Fun Gums Bag account. We work in teams and share ideas. We also use research to decide on the image and how to aim it correctly at the target market. "

● On task Investigate

Choose one sweet or chocolate wrapper aimed at young children and one aimed at adults. What is it about the wrappers that makes them more suitable for their target market?

Starting Point

As part of a mini-enterprise project you have been asked to make a flower holder. Can you design and batch-produce them and make a profit for your school and/or a charity?

How much...?

Have you ever stopped to think about all the different costs involved in making a product? The cost of the actual materials that have been used is usually only a small proportion. Labour, marketing and retail costs, and VAT account for a significant amount. These costs vary, depending on the product.

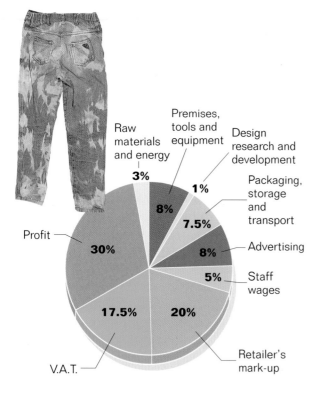

What's the cost of a pair of jeans?

Raw materials and energy — 3%
Premises, tools and equipment — 8%
Design research and development — 1%
Packaging, storage and transport — 7.5%
Advertising — 8%
Staff wages — 5%
Retailer's mark-up — 20%
V.A.T. — 17.5%
Profit — 30%

Cutting costs

Businesses aim to try to reduce their production costs as much as possible. This enables them to reduce the price their goods can be sold at, and increases their profits.

Two particular ways businesses can cut their costs are:

▷ to reduce the amount and/or quality of the raw materials they use
▷ to speed up the production process, so that more can be made in the same time.

Mini enterprise

As part of a mini-enterprise group you have been asked to design and make a batch product that will hold one or more flowers. They will be sold at local school fairs and possibly in local florist shops.

The ornamental flower holders should use a standard test tube to contain the flowers. You will need to design and make an attractive structure to hold the test tube. You can use any materials you wish.

It is expected that the flower holders will mostly be bought as presents, and that people might be willing to pay between £5 and £10 for such a product.

Initially you will design and make just one *prototype* product to test your idea. Then you must show how you could save on materials and production time if you were making them in quantity. Finally your group will work together to make a batch of ten.

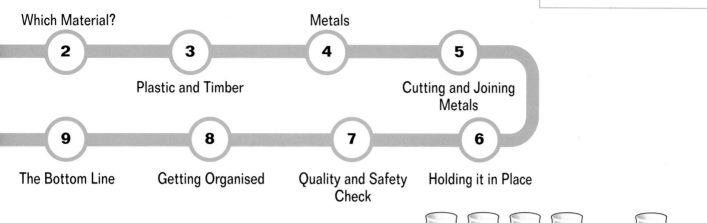

Which Material?

2

3

Plastic and Timber

Metals

4

5

Cutting and Joining
Metals

9

8

7

6

The Bottom Line

Getting Organised

Quality and Safety
Check

Holding it in Place

You might wish to propose an alternative product to design and make. You must get your teacher's approval to do this, however.

● *On task Investigate*

Look through books, magazines, catalogues, etc. to find images of flowers and flower holders. You might find pictures of candle holders useful too. If possible, look on the Internet as well. Record your findings on design sheet **1a**.

The challenge

The challenge is to design and make a number of identical, attractive products as quickly and cost-effectively as possible.

The focus

In this unit you will gain an understanding of the different methods of industrial production and how products are designed so they can be easily made. This is called **design for manufacture**.

You will need to explore ways to make your product more cheaply. At the same time though, it's got to be good enough quality for people to want to buy it. The appearance of the product, the ease and the method of manufacture will all effect how much money you could raise.

The end product

You need to:

▶ make a prototype of your product
▶ show how they could be made quickly and cheaply in quantity
▶ work as part of a team to produce a batch of products.

95

Understanding Production

1

Flower Power

Do you know about the different ways in which products are made? What's the difference between one-off, batch and mass production? How did it all start?

It's also time to start having some ideas for the design of your test-tube flower holder.

Design for manufacture

The way most things are made has changed considerably in the last 250 years. Up to the middle of the eighteenth century all products were individually made by highly skilled craftsmen and women.

During the Industrial Revolution many of the jobs done by craftspeople began to be done by automated machines instead. This meant that products could be made more quickly and in greater numbers, though they were not necessarily of as good quality.

During the early 1900s, the idea of making things on a production line was introduced. The idea was that each worker just made one part of a product as it passed down a conveyor belt or **assembly line**.

One of the first successfully mass-produced items was the *Model T* car, made by Henry Ford between 1908 and 1916. It was assembled on a production line by workers who did the same job all day.

Today robots carry out many of these repetitive tasks.

Production processes

Products can be manufactured in a number of different ways.

One-off production

This is the most costly method but does allow for a personalised product, such as a made-to-measure suit of clothes.

Batch production

This is used where a company needs to produce a limited number of the same product. It then changes its production line to make a different product. Using this method companies can respond quickly to market demand.

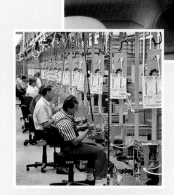

Mass production

Most common consumer products are made by mass production. Workers are organised to carry out individual tasks, where they become skilled and efficient. At times they are rotated around a number of tasks to keep their interest.

Standardised parts

Many products make use of standard parts. Look at different cars from the same manufacturer. You will see that there are many parts that are common across the model range. Examples are door handles and controls on the dashboard and steering wheels.

● *On task Investigate / Have good ideas*

1. Ask the science department if you can measure a range of test tubes. One of these will be a standard part that you will use in the design of your flower holder.

2. On design sheet **1b** complete a drawing showing the range of sizes that test tubes are available in. Write down which you think the best size will be.

3. On design sheet **1c** sketch your first ideas for possible holders for the test tube. Remember to add notes, and some colour.

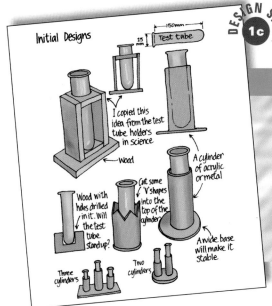

On your design sheets

- Collect images of flowers and candle holders. **1a**

- Show the sizes of test-tubes and say which you will use. **1b**

- Sketch some initial ideas. Add notes and colour. **1c**

Remember

- There are three different methods of production.

- Companies use standardised parts to help reduce costs.

Which Material?

2

Flower Power

Choosing which material to use for your design will be very important. What particular properties and characteristics will it need to have?

Properties and characteristics

All materials have different **properties**. Some materials may be very light, such as an aluminium alloy. While another, such as high tensile steel, may be very strong.

At the same time, each material has its own working **characteristics**.

This means how it can best be cut, joined, or finished. For example, plastics are very easy to mould into complex shapes. This has allowed designers to be very creative in their ideas.

In recent years there has been a growth in the use of modern composite materials. These materials have been specially manufactured to have particular properties and characteristics. For example, carbon fibre is used in the construction of Formula 1 racing cars. It is very strong, yet extremely lightweight, although also expensive.

Michael Schumacher wrecks his engine in the Australian Grand Prix, 1998.

Considerations in material selection

- Weight
- Cost
- Strength
- Methods of manufacture
- Scale of production
- Availability
- Finish and Aesthetics

● *On task 1 Apply what you know*

What material properties are important in the manufacture of the following products: washing-up bowl, milk crate, crash helmet, bicycle frame, household bath, soft drinks container, toothpaste tube? Record your answers in the table on design sheet **2a**.

Property checklist

Strength
The strength of a material is its ability to resist having its shape changed.
How strong does your design need to be?

Toughness
A material's toughness is measured by its ability to withstand impact.
How tough does your product need to be?

Brittleness
Brittle materials will break very suddenly, as they do not bend. Glass is a brittle material.

Hardness
A material is hard if it has the ability not to be scratched or damaged.
Which parts of your product might be most easily damaged?

Stiffness
A material's stiffness is its ability to withstand being bent.
Do any parts of your design need to be flexible?

Conductivity
Different materials allow electricity and heat to pass through.
Do you need a material that has a high or low level of conductivity?

● On task 2 Apply what you know

1. On design sheet **2b**, make a statement about the properties and characteristics your materials will need to have.

2. Suggest what you think the most suitable materials might be. Check if they are available to you in school. Also consider if you think you have the necessary skills to work with them?

On your design sheets

- Sketch some familiar products and list their material properties and characteristics. **2a**

- State what properties and characteristics your materials will need to have, and what the best materials to use might be. **2b**

Remember

- The correct choice of material is important in the design of any product and is an integral part of the design process.

- Modern product design has changed because of the growth of new materials that can be moulded into complex shapes.

Plastic and Timber

3

Flower Power

How suitable would plastic or timber
be for different parts
of your design?

Acrylic

Acrylic is a stiff, hard
thermoplastic. It can be cut easily,
drilled and bent. Pieces can then be
glued together using Tensol cement.
It is available in a wide range of
opaque and clear colours.
Acrylic is often known as
Perspex, which is a trade
name.

Using acrylic

A shape can be marked out using a
permanent OHP pen. This can be cleaned off at
the end. It is best to drill a small pilot hole first by
hand, then finish the hole to size on a drilling
machine. Then cut the shape and finish the edges.
The final task is to bend the acrylic and glue the
pieces together.

For batch production a series of templates and jigs
can be made to speed the making process up and
help ensure consistency.

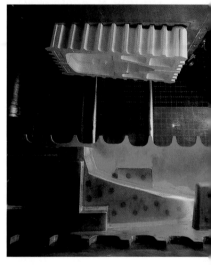

Vacuum forming

Many thermoplastics
are suitable for vacuum
forming (see pages
54–55). This process
enables them to be
moulded into the same
shape, and so is useful
for batch production.

Thermoset plastics	
Melamine formaldehyde	Hard and heat resistant. Used for kitchen worktops.
Urea formaldehyde	Used to make electrical fittings such as light switches.

Thermoplastics	
High density polythene (HDPE)	Quite strong. Used for household items such as washing-up bowls.
Low density polythene (LDPE)	Soft. Used for flexible containers such as washing-up liquid bottles.
Rigid polystyrene	Used for rigid cases, such as hi-fi's. It can be vacuum formed at school.

Timber

There are many different types of hardwood and softwood available. These often have great natural beauty, but can be very expensive. There are also manufactured boards, such as hardboard, plywood, chipboard and medium density fibreboard (often known as MDF). Each has different working properties.

Jigs and templates are useful when batch-producing a product that uses timber. A lathe can be used for creating complex circular forms.

Softwoods	Characteristics	Properties	Uses
Sitka spruce	Resists splitting but has resin pockets and knots fall out	Tough and durable but easy to work. Can be painted or varnished.	Building work, paper making, packing cases, low-cost furniture
Parana pine	Tough with a fine grain and few knots	Tends to shrink rapidly on drying and to twist. Suitable for jointed constructions.	Shelves, cupboards, fitted furniture, step ladders

Hardwoods	Characteristics	Properties	Uses
Mahogany	Hard and strong	Easy to work	Furniture, panelling, veneers
Beech	Hard and strong with close grain. Not suitable for outside use	Works easily. Good for turning on a lathe.	Furniture, toys, tools, kitchen utensils

● On task 1 Apply what you know

Find four products made from plastic and four made from timber. Sketch them on design sheet **3a** and say what types of plastic or wood they have each been made from.

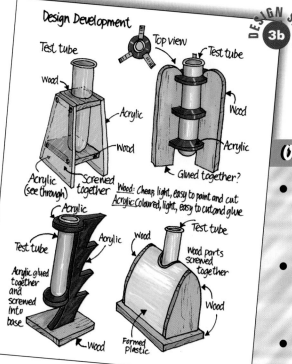

Design Development

● On task 2 Develop your design

1. On design sheet **3b** develop your ideas for your flower holder. Explain how your designs could be made. Explore how the different colours and textures of different materials and finishes could be combined to improve your flower holder's appearance.

2. Make a series of card models/mock-ups to test out your ideas in 3D. You might need to work at different scales, or use different materials that are cheaper – it all depends on what aspect of your design you are testing out. Modify your models until you are happy with the results. Describe what you did on design sheet **3c**.

On your design sheets

- Sketch a number of plastic and wooden products. Explain what type of plastic or wood has been used. **3a**

- Sketch a range of ideas. Explain your reasons for the type of material you have chosen to use. **3b**

- Describe the models you made. **3c**

Remember

- There are two types of plastic: thermoplastic and thermoset plastic.

- There are three types of wood: softwood, hardwood and manufactured board.

Metals

Another material you need to consider is metal.

There are two basic types of metal, **ferrous** and **non-ferrous**.

Ferrous metals contain iron and this will make them rust if they are not protected. This can be achieved by painting, plastic coating, enamelling or galvanising. Common ferrous metals include mild steel, cast iron, tool steel and tin plate.

Non-ferrous metals can be used for decorative purposes, such as jewellery. They are also used for more functional objects, such as electrical switches. Common non-ferrous metals include aluminium alloy, brass and copper.

Metals are available in a range of cross sectional shapes, as well as flat sheets.

Metals come from impure ores that are dug out of the ground. The ore is processed by heating it to a very high temperature in a blast furnace. Other materials can be added to the process to change the metal's properties. A metal changed in this way is called an **alloy**.

The converter in a blast furnace.

Ironwork can be highly decorative as well as functional. This Dragon Gate was designed in the late 1880s by the Spanish architect, Antonio Gaudi.

Use of metals

Mild steel

This is the most common ferrous metal. It is relatively soft, containing approximately 0.3% carbon. It can easily be shaped and formed.

It is used for car bodies, nuts and bolts, and furniture. It needs to be finished to protect it and improve its appearance.

Tool steel

This steel contains 1% carbon. It can be hardened so it can be used to make tools.

Cast iron

This is brittle iron. It is used to make vices and machine tools. It was used to make the first iron bridge, in the town of Iron Bridge in Shropshire.

Tin plate

A very thin layer of tin is used to protect the steel and stop it from rusting. It is used for tins of food, paint, etc.

Copper

This conducts electricity very well. It is quite soft. It is also used for water pipes, as it is easy to soft solder pieces together.

Brass

Copper and zinc are used to make this alloy. It is quite hard and can be used for decorative purposes.

Aluminium

In its pure form aluminium is very soft. It can be combined with other materials, such as copper, to form a lightweight, strong alloy. It can easily corrode. To prevent this it is anodised.

Aluminium is widely used in bicycles and aircraft.

Remember

- There are two basic types of metal, ferrous and non-ferrous.

- Metals have a wide range of different properties.

- Ferrous metals need to be finished to protect them and improve their appearance.

- A metal changed by adding another material is called an alloy.

● *On task Apply what you know*

1. Find six items that have been made from different metals. Draw them on design sheet **4a**. State the material and reasons for its use.

2. Draw a range of different cross sectional shapes of metals that can be found in your school's store. Draw them in a chart on design sheet **4b**.

Cutting and Joining Metals

5

Metals can be joined together by soldering, brazing and welding or by mechanical means, such as a nut and bolt or rivet. It is difficult to join different types of metals together.

Cutting metals

There are some special tools you will need to use for cutting metals.

Hacksaw

Try square

Steel wool

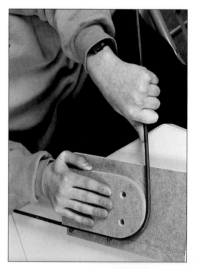

Callipers

Tin snips

Bending metals

Smaller section materials can be bent by hand. It is best to bend the metal around a **former**. Ask your teacher to show you how to do this. Larger sections may need to be warmed, so they become soft.

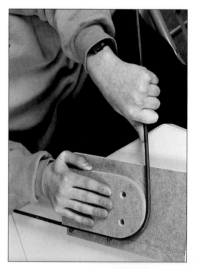

It is also possible to beat sheet material into curved shapes. As this process is carried out the metal becomes hard. It can be softened again by **annealing**.

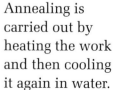

Annealing is carried out by heating the work and then cooling it again in water.

Using mechanical fasteners

It is easy to put a thread on to the end of round section material by using a die. A nut can then be used to hold different pieces together. See also page 57.

Rivets can be used to form a permanent joint. Holes are drilled in the two pieces that are to be joined. The holes are countersunk, before the rivet is hammered in place. The joint can then be filed, making the rivet almost invisible.

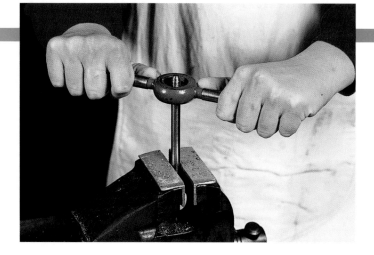

Brazing mild steel

This provides a strong joint between two pieces of mild steel. Clean the area to be brazed by filing or with emery cloth. Put some flux on the joint and place firebricks around the metal to hold the heat in.

It is a good idea to wire the pieces together so they do not move during the process. Heat the joint until it is red hot, and then touch the solder so it melts into the joint. Allow the joint to cool before it is placed into cold water.

● On task Apply what you know / Develop your design

1. Find four products where metals have been joined together. List them on design sheet **5a** and explain what processes have been used.

2. On design sheet **5b** develop your design. Think of using a range of material sizes and sections. Use notes and detail drawings to explain how you will join the pieces together.

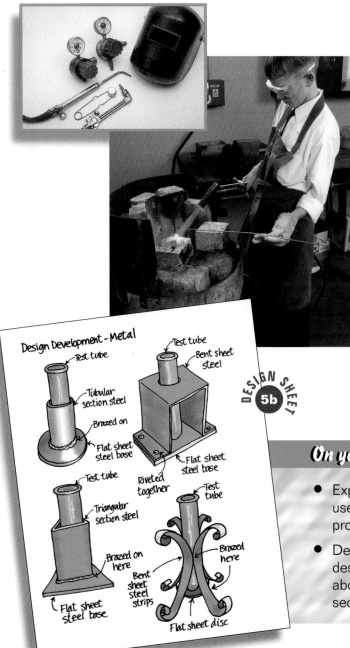

Design Development - Metal

Test tube
Test tube
Tubular section steel
Bent sheet steel
Brazed on
Flat sheet steel base
Flat sheet steel base
Test tube
Riveted together
Test tube
Triangular section steel
Brazed on here
Brazed here
Bent sheet steel strips
Flat sheet steel base
Flat sheet disc

DESIGN SHEET **5b**

On your design sheets

● Explain what metals have been used to make four different products. **5a**

● Develop your flower-holder design. Apply what you know about material sizes and sections. **5b**

Remember

● Metals can be joined by a variety of processes.

● Soldering, brazing, and welding form permanent joints.

● Non-permanent joints can be made by using nuts and bolts.

Holding it in Place

6

To ensure each product is made to the same size, you will need to use a range of jigs and fixtures.

Jigs and fixtures

A **jig** is used to drill a series of holes in exactly the same place on each piece. This helps ensure they all fit together accurately when assembled. You might be able to use a simple jig to help locate any holes in identical components in your product.

In industry a jig is normally made from mild steel. A special collar, called a hardened bush, is fitted to the holes in the template. These help prevent wear. They can be easily replaced if damaged.

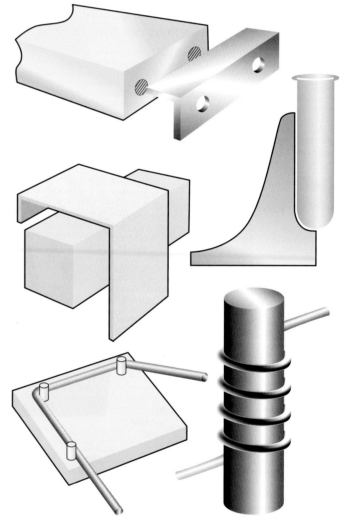

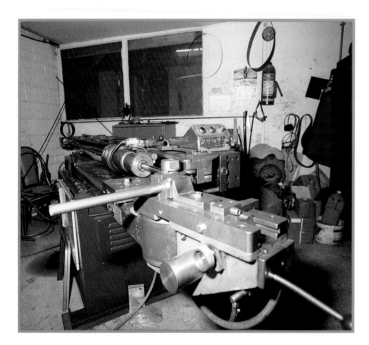

A **fixture** is a specially designed clamp or holding device. It is used when an item is to be worked on and especially useful when it is a complex shape.

● *On task 1 Develop your design*

Look at the design of your product. On design sheet **6a** show where the use of a jig or fixture might help speed up the production process and help produce consistent results. You could make a template or a jig to help bend pieces of acrylic to the same angle.

CNC tools

Computer Numerically Controlled (CNC) machine tools are programmed so they produce a range of components. The programme can be changed at any time to make a different sized component. This makes them flexible and they can be used to customise products.

You may have a CNC machine tool at school. It might be ideal to cut out some of the parts of your product.

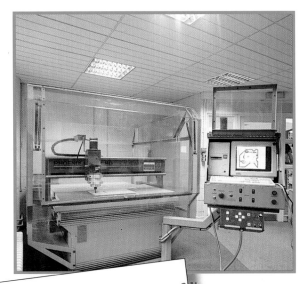

DESIGN SHEET 6a

Jigs and Fixtures

Bend
Bend
Bent sheet steel
Bend
Bend
Bend
Riveted
Flat sheet steel

Bend

Former held in a vice

Steel strips need to be bent at the end to make these curls

Mole grips hold the steel strip in place

Former held in a vice

Steel strip is bent around former

● On task 2 Evaluate / Develop your design

1. Review your design. Are there ways you could change it so it would be easier to make? Draw these modifications on design sheet **6b** and explain how you can incorporate them into your product.

2. On design sheet **6b**, explain how you could use a CNC machine to customise your product.

On your design sheets

- Show how you could use a jig or fixture to improve your production process. **6a**

- Explain how your product could be re-designed so it would be easier to make. **6b**

- Describe how you could use a CNC machine. **6b**

Remember

- Jigs and fixtures are used in industry to help produce consistently sized components.

- CNC machine tools can be used in a flexible way to produce a range of different sized components.

Quality and Safety Checks

Products need to be of a consistent quality. Each needs to be as good as another. How could you check the quality of your product as it is being made?

Quality control

You need to ensure that your final product is made to the highest quality. To achieve this a system of **quality control** is needed. This system will check the quality of the products as they are being made.

Quality checks could include:

▷ ensuring the raw materials are acceptable
▷ measuring sizes of parts after they have been marked out and cut out
▷ checking how well different parts fit together
▷ seeing if surface finishes are adequately applied
▷ looking for marks or other imperfections on the final product.

In industry

In industry a sample of components or operations are inspected during the production process. Computers play a central part in collecting and analysing test data.

Good quality control helps identify potential problems before they stop the manufacturing process.

Sometimes special tools or templates need to be made to help check the product is being made accurately.

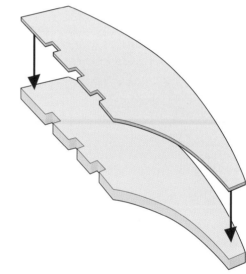

British Standards

The **British Standards Institute** helps promote quality by producing documents that clarify the essential technical requirements for a product, material or process. There are over 10,000 British Standards that cover almost every product in our lives, from the food we eat to the construction of our homes.

Look for the BS Kite mark and its European equivalent on the products you buy.

This ensures that an acceptable quality can be expected.

Making it safely

A production line can be a dangerous place, especially if power tools or dangerous chemicals are being used. It's important to ensure that those working on the production line follow the necessary safety guidelines and regulations. These might be concerned with:

▷ wearing protective clothing

▷ handling materials

▷ using hand and machine tools.

Each stage of the production process needs to be analysed for potential hazards. Appropriate safety precautions need to be built into the overall production plan.

In addition to quality control checks, regular safety checks need to be made.

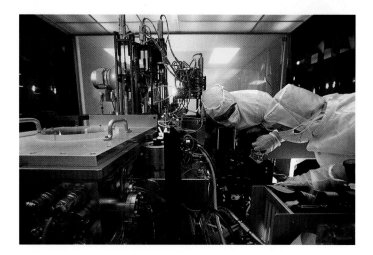

● On task 1 Apply what you know

Find three different products that have some form of safety mark. Draw them on design sheet **7a** and explain what safety issue they are warning about.

● On task 2 Plan the making

1. On design sheet **7b** write a list of the main stages of making your product. Identify the processes involved at each step. Add in the checks for quality you could make at different points. For example:

Step 16. Cut out base plate. *Use ruler to check slot is at least 10mm.*

2. Record ideas for a special item (e.g. a template) to help check quickly the quality of one of the components or processes in your products.

3. On design sheet **7c** list and explain potential safety hazards in the making of your product. Consider clothing, materials and tools.

Safety Marks

DESIGN SHEET 7a

This label was found on a can of Spray Mount.

It is telling you that the contents of the can are extremely flammable.

This label was found on a container for white spirit.

It is telling you that the contents of the container are harmful to the environment.

On your design sheets

● Draw and explain three safety marks or symbols. **7a**

● List the steps of making your product. Add in quality checks. **7b**

● Show your ideas for using special tools or templates. **7b**

● Identify safety precautions and checks needed in your production process. **7c**

Remember

● Quality control systems check the manufacturing process at different stages.

● Regular checks for safety are essential.

Getting Organised

Once you have finalised your design and have identified quality and safety checks, you need to plan how it is going to be made in large quantities.

Production planning

Industrial companies spend a lot of time planning the manufacturing process. Time spent in this process will save time and money later. In industry, a Production Engineer completes this job.

Complex flow-charts are drawn up to ensure that all the materials, components and the product being made, arrive in the right place at the right time. They are also used to help plan a work schedule that makes sure no-one is waiting for something to do.

Sometimes parts of a product are made separately, and then fed into the production line. These are known as **sub-assemblies**.

In industry these symbols are used to identify different types of operation in the production process.

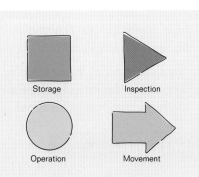

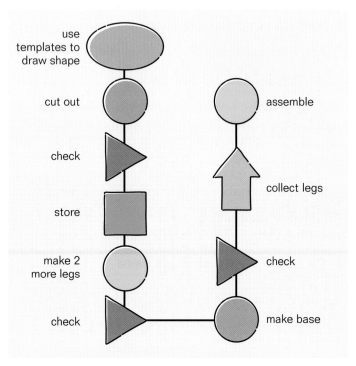

On task 1
Plan the making / Work with materials

1. Look back at design sheets **7b** and **7c**. Use the symbols above to turn your list of manufacturing steps into a flow-chart for making your product. Do this on design sheet **8a**.

2. Make up your final design, following your flow-chart. Record how long each step takes to complete.

Testing the market

Once you have designed and made a prototype product you can test the market one lunchtime at school.

● On task 2 Evaluate / Develop your design

Ask people what they think of your product.

▶ Would they buy it?

▶ How much would they be prepared to pay for it?

▶ Can they suggest any improvements?

It's still not too late to modify your design if you do not think it will sell too well. Record your findings, and show any changes you make on design sheet **8b**.

● On task 3 Plan the making

When you have finalised your design you need to work out how a team of people could make a batch of the products as quickly and efficiently as possible.

▶ If one operation takes a long time, several people might work on it at once.

▶ A part of the product could be made as a sub-assembly.

▶ Someone could be checking the whole process to make sure it is running as smoothly as possible.

Remember to add in quality-control check points and safety procedures and to allocate people to do these jobs. Record your plans on design sheet **8c**.

Getting in line

When all the operations have been identified, you will need to plan the layout of the production line. You will not be able to move the machines in the school workshop but you will need to consider where some of the other activities are carried out.

In industry this process is usually completed on a computer. The computer can then simulate the manufacturing process to check it works.

Robot vehicles transport drums of oil around a chemical plant.

● On task 4 Plan the making

1. Draw a plan of your school workshop on design sheet **8d**.

2. Use different coloured lines and symbols to show the production route. Make sure they are the correct ones.

● On task 5
Plan the making / Work with materials

1. Working with your team, make a batch of ten of your product. Follow your production plan closely. Time how long it takes.

2. Record the results of the quality inspections during the production process. You can use this information to help identify areas that are causing problems.

3. After your team has made ten of your product, stop the process. Ask everyone what problems there have been. Record what happened on design sheet **8e**.

4. Modify your plan to improve the production process.

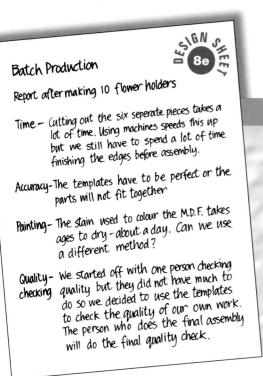

DESIGN SHEET 8e

Batch Production

Report after making 10 flower holders

Time – Cutting out the six seperate pieces takes a lot of time. Using machines speeds this up but we still have to spend a lot of time finishing the edges before assembly.

Accuracy – The templates have to be perfect or the parts will not fit together

Painting – The stain used to colour the M.D.F. takes ages to dry – about a day. Can we use a different method?

Quality checking – We started off with one person checking quality but they did not have much to do so we decided to use the templates to check the quality of our own work. The person who does the final assembly will do the final quality check.

On your design sheets

● Draw up a detailed production plan for your product. **8a**

● Say what happened when you tested the market. **8b**

● Explain how a team of people could make your product. **8c**

● Show the plan for your production line. **8d**

● Describe what happened during production. **8e**

Remember

● Production planning is an important part of the manufacturing process. It is vital to the success of a company.

The Bottom Line

How many of your products do you need to sell to make a profit? What price are people prepared to pay for it?

Costing your product

How much would it cost to make a batch of 100 of your product? To calculate this you will need to work out the total amount of materials and components required.

Making a profit

The profit you make on each product you sell can be easily worked out by subtracting the cost of manufacture from the selling price. If something costs £4 to make and is sold for £5, the profit is £1.

Suppose it costs £300 to make 100 products in a batch. If you sold all of them for £5 each, the profit would be £2 each – or £200 if you sold them all. But what if you sold only 50 at £5 each? Instead of a profit, there would be a loss of £50 (i.e. £300 minus £250).

The point at which the total number sold is equal to the cost of manufacture is called the **bottom line**. Before you invest in your materials, you need to be confident that you will sell enough to cover your costs.

One way of reducing the cost of manufacture is to reduce the amount of waste material. Look carefully at the size and shape of the pieces of your product. How many of these are being cut out from one sheet of material? Could they be re-arranged or re-designed so more pieces could be cut from a single sheet?

● On task 1 Investigate

Use trade catalogues to find prices for the materials and components you would need – remember products are usually cheaper if you buy them in bulk. Don't forget to include delivery to your workshop!

For this task you do not need to include the costs of labour, energy, etc., but you should include any other expenses that will need to be paid for. Work out your costings on design sheet **9a**. Use a spreadsheet if you can, as it will make it easier to work out how to reduce the costs.

What would be the effect on the unit cost and bottom line if you made 1,000 identical products instead?

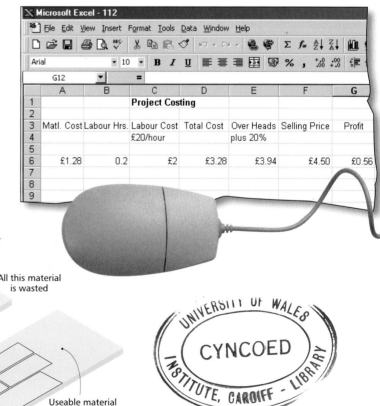

All this material is wasted

Easier to cut out

Useable material left over

● On task 2 Final evaluation

1. Look at the design of your product. How could it be modified or changed to improve its appeal? Maybe it could be used for more than one purpose, for example also as a pencil holder or bookend, perhaps? Sketch your ideas on design sheet **9b**.

2. Show your new ideas to the rest of your group. What do they think of them? Record their comments on design sheet **9b**, and say if you agree with them.

● On task 3 Develop your design

How could you improve the image and appeal of your product by designing a package for it?
This is especially important if it is being bought as a present. Show your ideas on design sheet **9c**.

● On task 4 Final evaluation

1. Read 'An interview with... Dyson' on the next page.

2. Imagine you are being interviewed for a local newspaper about how you designed your flower holder. What answers would you give to similar questions about how you developed your design ideas? Write your answers down on design sheet **9d**. Include some illustrations.

DESIGN SHEET 9d

Question 1
Where did you get your idea from?

Answer
We looked at the types of flower holders we had at home. We also looked in shops, magazines, books and catalogues. We tried to make our design futuristic.

Question 2
Can you describe some of the ways you check the quality of the product.

Answer
We made very accurate templates so we could check the quality of our work. We made sure that our work was accurate so that there was less waste and we saved money in time and materials.

Template 1

Template 2

On your design sheets

- Explain how your product could be costed. **9a**

- Make suggestions to improve your product. **9b**

- Say how other people responded to your suggestions. **9b**

- Sketch ideas for packaging your product. **9c**

- Explain how you developed your design ideas. **9d**

Remember

- The total selling price must cover all the costs.

- Try to reduce the material waste and overhead costs.

An Interview with...

In 1993 James Dyson launched the first Dyson Dual Cyclone vacuum cleaner. Since then they have become the fastest selling vacuum cleaners ever to have been made. What's the secret of their success?

dual cyclone TECHNOLOGY

dyson

What made you want to design a new vacuum cleaner? Where did you get the idea from?

66 I realised there was a problem with a bag vacuum cleaner because it clogged and blocked the air flow. I discovered a system called a cyclone. These are ten feet tall and sit on the top of saw mills.

The *eureka* moment was realising that a cyclone could separate the dust and dirt without putting anything in the way of the air. This principle was then applied to the development of a new approach to the design of a vacuum cleaner 99

Right: a traditional bag vacuum cleaner is adapted to become a prototype.

Since then you've designed a range of cleaners. How have you set about this?

66 We begin by thinking of several different ideas for a new product. These are quickly sketched.

From this we write a design specification – a list of all the key design features we want to include. 99

DCO2 DESIGN SPECIFICATION

Performance
The product – a cylinder vacuum cleaner – will exceed the performance of competitors in relevant tests e.g. IEC standard tests for dust pick up, filtration and air watts. It will use Dyson Dual Cyclone™ technology.

Ergonomics
It will be light, easy to move and should hug the stairs.

Aesthetics
Size, shape, proportions, balance amd colour will emphasise the function and will be in keeping with the DCO1.

Maintenence
It will be easy to empty and clean.

Context/environment
Where it will be kept and how it will be treated (in cupboards, pulled into furniture, knocked down the starirs) means that it will be reliable, robust and durable. Shock resistant meterials like ABS will be used.

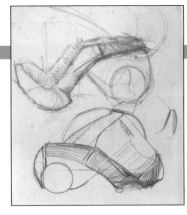

Design sketches

Working prototype

Foam model

Hand built model

What happens next?

❝ Hundreds of different prototype models are made. These enable us to test out how well our ideas work. They also give an impression of how the product might look. We use lots of different materials to make the prototype models. For example:

▷ cardboard models provide a quick and easy way of working out what the different component parts are

▷ working models show how well it might perform

▷ foam models are best for developing shapes and forms. ❞

The colours and shapes of the components help to identify the position and operation of various catches and switches.

Can you describe some of the ways you check the quality of the products being manufactured?

❝ Most of the parts are injection moulded. It's important to check that there are no imperfections. The sort of things we look out for are:

Flash – wafer thin material where two halves of the mould join

Split line – a fine line where two halves of the mould join

Feed point – this marks where the material flowed into the tool

Sinkage – uneven surfaces usually found above a rib

Distortion – a large area of the part is twisted or bowed.

The accuracy of the moulded parts we make means that many of the components fit together easily. This reduces manufacturing costs considerably. Finally the cleaners are packaged up and distributed across the world. ❞

● On task Investigate

1. Who first invented the vacuum cleaner and when? See if you can find out.

2. Find a range of products that include plastic components that have been injection moulded. Can you find any of the manufacturing defects described above?

Starting Point

Charities raise money for good causes. Can you design and make a money box that will encourage young children to insert coins?

There are many different charitable causes. Many of them aim to raise money to help disadvantaged people and animals around the world.

Charities raise money in many different ways. One long-established method has been to provide special money boxes that are placed on shop counters. The aim is to encourage customers to donate their small change.

Oxfam

Oxfam *helps people in under-developed countries.*

Help the Aged

Help the Aged *cares for elderly people who are unable to look after themselves.*

The Disabled Foundation *exists to support those with severe mental or physical handicaps.*

Registered charity no. 219099

The RSPCA helps animals.

Many charities want to try to encourage younger children to give money. To do this they need a money box that has a novelty feature – in other words, something happens when a coin is inserted.

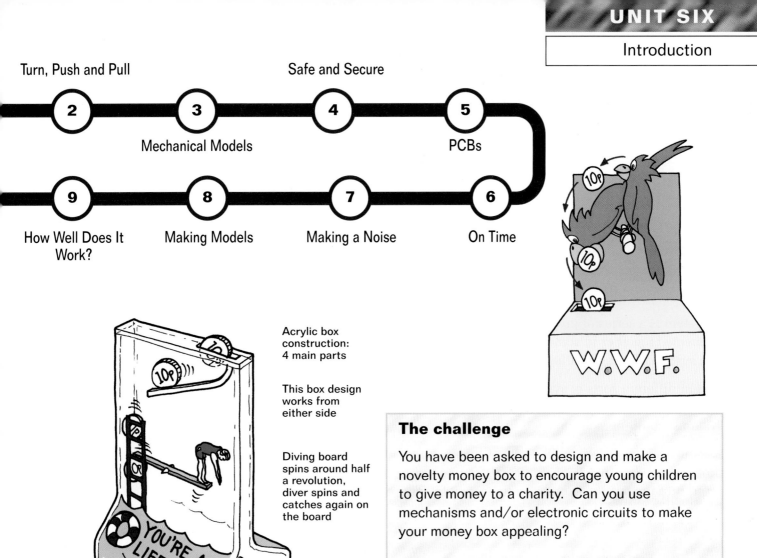

Turn, Push and Pull

Safe and Secure

(2) — (3) — (4) — (5)

Mechanical Models

PCBs

(9) — (8) — (7) — (6)

How Well Does It Work?

Making Models

Making a Noise

On Time

Acrylic box construction: 4 main parts

This box design works from either side

Diving board spins around half a revolution, diver spins and catches again on the board

Words, sea and ladder printed in reverse on the inside of the acrylic

Money collection box, locked panel underneath

YOU'RE A LIFESAVER

THANK YOU

W.W.F.

● On task Investigate / Apply what you know

1. On design sheet **1a** list six different charities and explain what cause they support.

2. Choose one charity. Plan a number of things you could do to find out more about it. For example:

► contacting its local branch
► visiting its shop, if it has one
► using the internet
► interviewing someone who works for it.

Record what you discover on design sheet **1b**.

3. Write a detailed design specification for a suitable money box. Include requirements for use, size, shape, weight, safety, durability, finish, etc. Do this on design sheet **1c**.

The challenge

You have been asked to design and make a novelty money box to encourage young children to give money to a charity. Can you use mechanisms and/or electronic circuits to make your money box appealing?

The focus

Mechanisms and electronics are widely used in everyday products. You will gain a greater understanding of how some of these work and how you can apply what you know in your project work.

You will also need to develop your understanding of systems and control.

As you work, try to apply as much as you can about what you already know of materials, components, tools and processes.

The end product

You will need to make a working money box. To judge its success you will need to find out:

► what other people think of your design

► how well it attracts children's attention.

1

What is a System?

To design mechanisms and electronic circuits you need to understand how to design systems. So what is a system? Can you identify the systems used in some familiar everyday products?

A system is a series of products or events that are connected together in some way. Changing one part of a system affects the other parts.

Lots of different sorts of systems have been designed, such as, transport systems, central heating systems, computer systems and hi-fi systems.

Systems can be described in terms of their inputs, processes and outputs. The process changes the input into the output. Controls are needed to ensure the process works effectively.

Inputs are the things that go together to make up the system.

The process is what happens to the inputs to change them into outputs.

Systems diagrams

Block diagrams are used to show the main features of a system. Complex systems may need many blocks to explain their operation.

For example, a simplified block diagram of a central heating system might look like this:

Input	Process	Output
Boiler Radiators Water pump Energy Temperature sensor	Water is heated and pumped around the system.	Temperature in room rises.

Feedback control

Has room reached required temperature? If so, switch off.

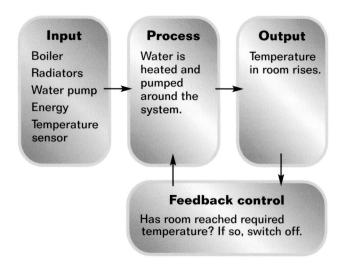

Outputs are the things that have been changed by the system.

Each block in the diagram is called a **sub-system**.

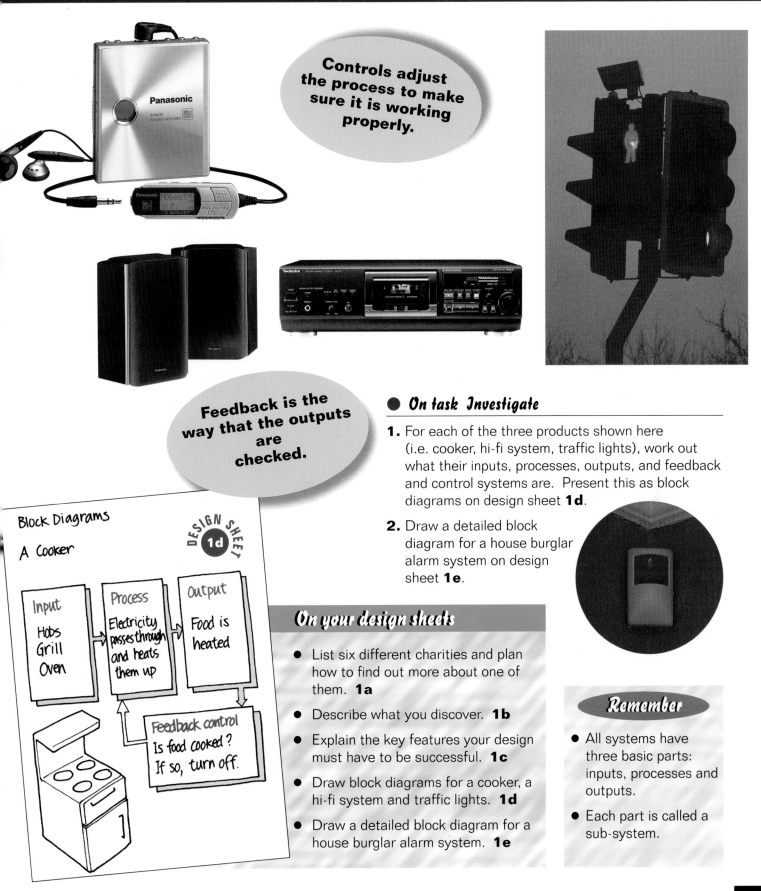

> Controls adjust the process to make sure it is working properly.

> Feedback is the way that the outputs are checked.

Block Diagrams

A Cooker

DESIGN SHEET **1d**

Input	Process	Output
Hobs Grill Oven	Electricity passes through and heats them up	Food is heated

Feedback control
Is food cooked?
If so, turn off.

● On task Investigate

1. For each of the three products shown here (i.e. cooker, hi-fi system, traffic lights), work out what their inputs, processes, outputs, and feedback and control systems are. Present this as block diagrams on design sheet **1d**.

2. Draw a detailed block diagram for a house burglar alarm system on design sheet **1e**.

On your design sheets

- List six different charities and plan how to find out more about one of them. **1a**

- Describe what you discover. **1b**

- Explain the key features your design must have to be successful. **1c**

- Draw block diagrams for a cooker, a hi-fi system and traffic lights. **1d**

- Draw a detailed block diagram for a house burglar alarm system. **1e**

> **Remember**
> - All systems have three basic parts: inputs, processes and outputs.
> - Each part is called a sub-system.

Turn, Push and Pull

2

Mechanisms change one type of motion into another type. Using a mechanism in your charity money box will help to make it interesting.

Types of motion

There are four types of motion: linear, rotary, reciprocating and oscillating motion.

Linear motion is movement in a straight line.

Rotary motion is movement that keeps on going round and round.

Oscillating motion – this swings at a steady rate, as found on a clock pendulum.

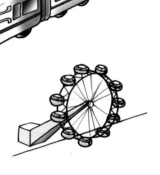

Reciprocating motion – this moves backwards and forwards, as found on an automatic door.

The lever

The lever is one of the oldest forms of mechanism. It is very simple and magnifies the force that is applied to it. The lever is found in many everyday products.

Classes of lever

All levers consist of the same four main parts: a beam, a load, an effort and a fulcrum (or pivot). There are three classes of lever; each has the **fulcrum**, **effort** and **load** arranged in a different order.

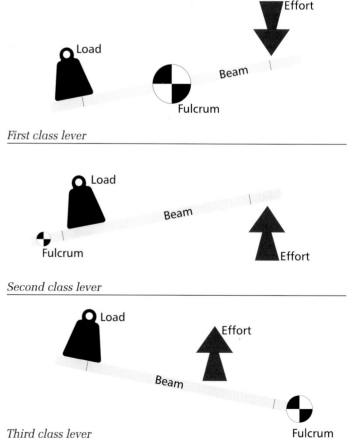

First class lever

Second class lever

Third class lever

120

Cranks

The simplest form of a **crank** is a wheel with a handle on it. A bicycle uses two cranks, which have pedals on them. If a linkage is connected to a crank it can be used to convert rotary motion into a reciprocating motion.

The distance between the centre of the wheel and the handle is called the **throw**. The linkage moves twice the throw of the crank.

When a crank is used with a linkage we call this a **crank/slider mechanism**.

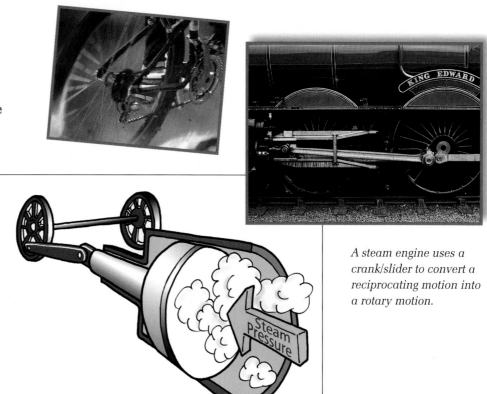

A steam engine uses a crank/slider to convert a reciprocating motion into a rotary motion.

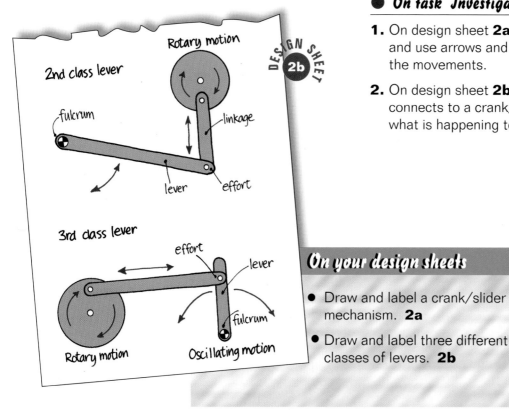

● *On task Investigate*

1. On design sheet **2a** draw a crank/slider mechanism and use arrows and labels on your drawing to show the movements.

2. On design sheet **2b** draw each class of lever so it connects to a crank/slider mechanism. Explain what is happening to the output motion.

On your design sheets

- Draw and label a crank/slider mechanism. **2a**

- Draw and label three different classes of levers. **2b**

Remember

- There are three different classes of lever.

- A crank can be used to convert rotary motion into a reciprocating motion.

- A crank and linkage is called a crank/slider mechanism.

Mechanical Models

3

It's difficult to design a successful mechanical system on paper. You need to make some working models and, if possible, use a computer. This will enable you to test your ideas out before you make the final version.

Your money box will have a backboard that you can incorporate a mechanism in. The input motion will come from a crank.

Rotary motion

Input crank

Money waiting to be knocked

Backboard

DESIGN SHEET 3a

● On task 1 Have good ideas

1. On design sheet **3a** sketch ideas for a mechanism that will then knock the money into the collection box. Look back at your previous sketches (design sheet **2a** and **b**). Consider how other mechanical products you have seen work. Use these to help you draw some ideas for your mechanism and explain the movement that will knock the money.

2. Add notes and further sketches to suggest how you can reflect your chosen charity in the design of the mechanism.

● On task 2 Develop your design

1. Decide on the size your backboard should be and cut a piece of card the same size.

2. Make a full size card model to check your mechanism will work.

3. Find out how you might be able to use CAD to help.

4. Record the results of your tests and experiments on design sheet **3b**. Discuss the suitability of the materials and components.

lever coins

The money sits on the lever which is moved by the crank, the money then slides into the box.

fulcrum

crank

backboard

The crank moves the slider which pushes the money into the box

coins

crank linkage

DESIGN SHEET 3a

● On task 3 Develop your design

1. Accurately draw the final design of your mechanism on design sheet **3c**. Show where the money will go and then drop.

2. On design sheet **3c** also draw the system diagram for your final design. Use colour on this diagram and the drawing of your final idea to show the input – process – output.

Making it move

It is important that all the parts in any mechanism are accurately made. If they are inaccurate the mechanism will not work correctly.

Modern computer controlled machines can manufacture thousands of identical parts using computer-aided manufacture (CAM). This means that the parts can be assembled without further checking.

Computer-aided design (CAD) software speeds up the design process. It can be used to model and test a design before it is actually made.

Making it eye-catching

● On task 4 Have good ideas

1. Design an eye-catching appearance for the backboard to draw attention to your money box. This will need to reflect your chosen charity and incorporate the design of your money box. You can use a computer graphics package to do this. Record your ideas on design sheet **3d**.

2. When you have finalised your idea draw the outline of the backboard full size.

3. Mark the position of any holes that will need to be drilled.

● On task 5 Work with materials

1. Make your mechanism as accurately as possible. Carefully measure your model and transfer these sizes to the final pieces.

2. Drill any holes in the backboard before you glue your graphic work in place. This can be covered with clear adhesive plastic to further enhance its appearance and prevent the mechanism from damaging it.

3. Push a plastic bush into the backboard to ensure the crank will turn smoothly.

4. On design sheet **3e** accurately draw and dimension the pieces of your mechanism. Explain about any difficulties you had while making the mechanism, and how you overcame them.

DESIGN SHEET 3e

110

55

25

Lever

Linkage Fulcrum

110

55

20

Crank

Problems with the mechanism
I found the crank really hard to make so I used a pre-made M.D.F. wheel instead

---

On your design sheets

- Sketch ideas for a mechanism. **3a**

- Describe and evaluate the models you tested. **3b**

- Draw your final mechanism accurately. **3c**

- Draw a system diagram. **3c**

- Design the backboard for your design. **3d**

- Draw and dimension the pieces of your mechanism. **3e**

Remember

- Designers use models to check the appearance and operation of their ideas before they are made.

- Computer-aided design (CAD) is used to help speed up the design process by modelling the designers' ideas before they are made.

Safe and Secure

4

Next you need to work out how the money can be securely contained in the box once it has been knocked in by the mechanism.

How could the front of the box be made more eye-catching?

Keeping it safe and secure

Some products need to be sold in secure containers, for example, paint and oil. Other products, such as food, often also include tamper-proof lids. These provide a visual indication that the container has not been opened.

● On task 1 Investigate

Find three tamper proof containers. Draw these on design sheet **4a** and explain how the tamper proof device works. Why do food packages have this type of top?

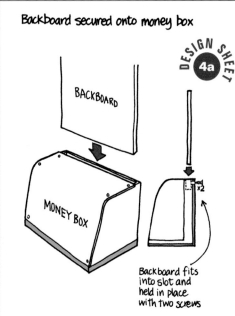

Backboard secured onto money box

DESIGN SHEET **4a**

BACKBOARD

MONEY BOX

Backboard fits into slot and held in place with two screws

It's in the box

The backboard you have designed and made needs to be attached to the money box. How this is achieved will depend on your choice of material. One method would be to use 12 mm thick pine for the box and incorporate two slots for the backboard to slide into.

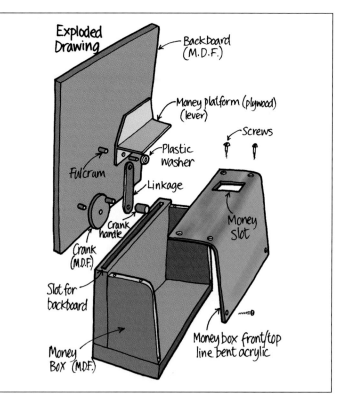

Exploded Drawing

Backboard (M.D.F.)

Money platform (plywood) (lever)

Screws

Fulcrum

Plastic washer

Linkage

Crank handle

Money Slot

Crank (M.D.F.)

Slot for backboard

Money Box (M.D.F.)

Money box front/top line bent acrylic

The width of your backboard will decide the size of the box. Ask your teacher to show you how to cut the slots in the end pieces of your box.

The top piece will need a slot in it so the money will fall into the box. This could be made from sheet material such as MDF or acrylic.

Looking different?

You could change the appearance of your box by sloping the front.

Can you think of any other ways of making the box look more unusual?

● On task 2
Have good ideas / Work with materials

1. Sketch some possible ideas for the front of your box on design sheet **4b**.

2. Make a card template for the design of the front to the box. Use this to check its appearance when the backboard is in place. You could use a single piece of acrylic and bend it, so it forms the top and front of the box.

3. Finish the front with paint or a scanner/cutter.

4. Check all the pieces fit correctly together before they are securely assembled by gluing or using screws.

5. On design sheet **4c** complete a series of drawings to show how your money box is made. Could someone else make your design from your instructions?

On your design sheets

● Explain how tamper proof devices work. **4a**

● Sketch ideas for the front of the box. **4b**

● Show how your money box is made. **4c**

Remember

● Many products are sold in tamper proof, secure containers.

● Check all the parts to a product fit correctly before you fix them together.

PCBs

5

As well as using a mechanism, an electronic circuit could be included. This could be used to attract people's attention or form an additional novelty feature, which is started when the money is dropped into the box.

Circuit boards

Electronic components are usually placed on a circuit board. This replaces wires with copper track and keeps all the components together. There are several ways of making these.

Making a circuit board

Temporary circuits can be modelled on a **prototype board**. These are sometimes known as **breadboards**, or **Veroboard**.

The legs of the components can be pushed into the holes in the board. They are then connected by clips at the back of the holes.

If components need to be fixed away from the board they are put on *flying leads*. These are wires attached to the circuit board with the components fixed to the ends.

Printed circuit boards

When the circuit has been finalised a permanent circuit can be made. There are two ways this can be done. One way is to use **stripboard.** This is similar to a prototype board. It is a plastic sheet with a grid of holes linked by copper strips.

The other method is to produce a **PCB**, or **printed circuit board**. First a mask needs to be drawn out full size on a piece of acetate.

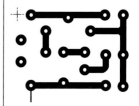

This is then exposed to ultra violet (UV) light and developed using chemicals. The circuit is then etched into a piece of copper.

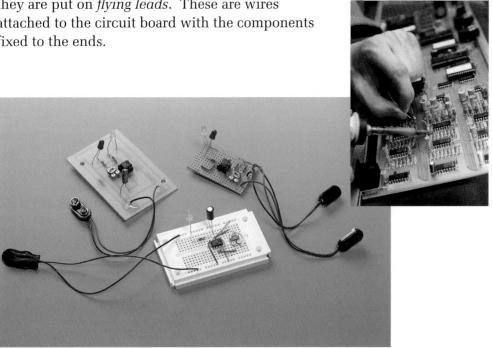

Next, holes are drilled to hold the electronic components, which are soldered on.

Assembling PCBs is a repetitive process. In industry robotic devices are used.

Inputs

Sensors can be used to control automatic systems. These act as **input** devices.

▷ A light dependent resistor (LDR) will sense light.

▷ A thermistor will sense heat.

▷ A moisture sensor will sense moisture.

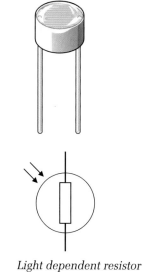 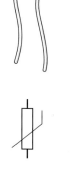

Light dependent resistor   *Thermistor*   *Moisture sensor*

You can use sensors with a transistor (see page 130) to make an automatic control system. These can be modelled on a computer or by using system boards.

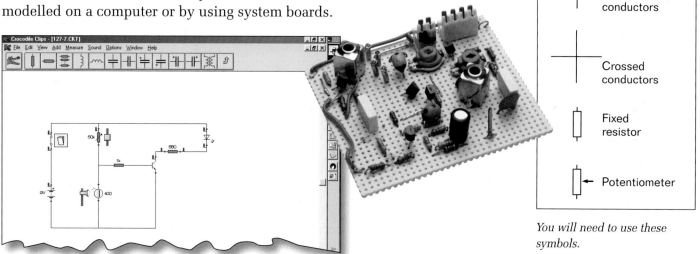

	Joined conductors
	Crossed conductors
	Fixed resistor
	Potentiometer

You will need to use these symbols.

● On task 1 Apply what you know

Your teacher will show you how to make a PCB. On design sheet **5** draw a sequential drawing of this process. You may need to practise this before making one for your final money box.

On your design sheet

● Show the main stages of how a PCB is made. **5**

Remember

● An input sensor needs to be used with a transistor to switch the output on.

● There are several ways of making an electronic circuit. A PCB is the most robust and is easy to mass produce.

6

On Time

You could add LEDs and an electronic timing device to your money box. It would start when the money is dropped in, so the LEDs light up for a set period of time.

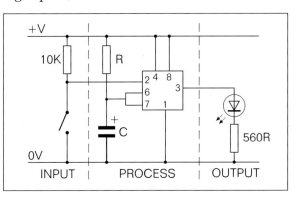

What's the time?

For a more interesting effect, you could use an electronic timing device. This could make the LEDs light up for a set amount of time when the money is dropped in.

Electronic timers have now replaced older mechanical ones. They are smaller, cheaper to make and more accurate. Electronic timing devices are found in microwave ovens, alarm clocks and video recorders.

Using an integrated circuit (IC)

ICs or *micro-chips* form the central part of all modern electronic circuits. These are normally rectangular and have a number of *legs* or pins that are connected to complete the circuit.

The IC is normally inserted in a holder which has already been soldered in place. This is because the IC can be very sensitive and soldering can damage it.

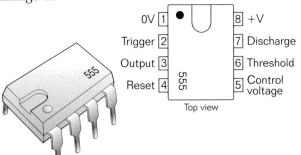

555

The 555 timer IC can be used to make a timer that, once triggered, will come on for a set period of time. This is called a **monostable** timer. The 555 IC has eight pins, numbered 1 to 8.

The timer is started when the switch is momentarily depressed. The output comes on for the timed period and then switches off. The length of time is controlled by the value of the resistor and capacitor.

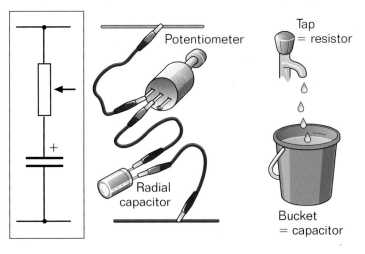

A potentiometer controls the flow of electricity, just like a tap controls the flow of water.

LEDs

LEDs are available in a range of colours and some will automatically flash. These have a small black dot in them. By using one flashing LED in series with a normal LED, both will flash. If you haven't used an LED before, look back at pages 36–37.

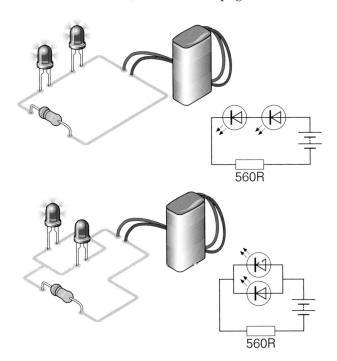

560R

560R

● On task 1 Develop your design

1. On design sheet **6a** show how you could use up to three LEDs in your design. Where could they be placed? Will any flash?

2. Draw the circuit diagram to show how your LEDs will need to be connected. Indicate what colour you will use.

3. Solder the components together and test your circuit.

On your design sheets

- Show how LEDs could be used in your design. **6a**

- Draw a timing circuit incorporating your LED circuit. **6b**

● On task 2 Develop your design

1. On design sheet **6b**, draw the timing circuit so it incorporates the LED circuit you have already made. Decide how long you want the LEDs to come on for when the money has been dropped in.

2. Use the table below to decide what value of resistor and capacitor you will need. Choose a preset resistor that is slightly larger than you need. This can be finely adjusted to set the time period accurately.

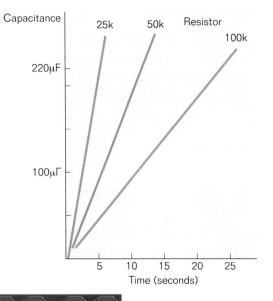

Remember

- Integrated circuits (ICs) form the central part of electronic circuits.

- Monostable timers come on for a set period of time and then switch off.

- Capacitors store electrical charge.

- A preset can be adjusted to give the required amount of resistance.

DESIGN SHEET 6a

HELP SAVE THE SEALS

LED's

7

Making a Noise

Integrated circuits can be designed to switch on other outputs apart from LEDs. You could consider using other outputs in your circuit.

Using other outputs

Integrated circuits can be designed to switch on a variety of outputs. An **output** device will use a signal from the **process** part of a system and convert it into movement, sound, heat or light.

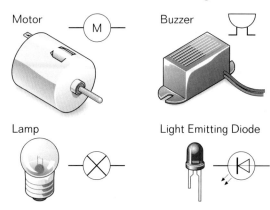

Using a transistor and a diode

The output current from an IC is very small, so you must use a transistor as part of the output of the circuit.

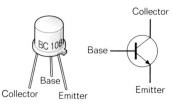

A transistor has three legs and works as a switch. A small current flows to the base leg of the transistor. This will switch the transistor on and allow a larger current to flow from the collector to the emitter.

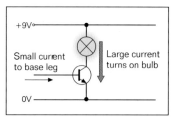

You must also use a diode, wired in parallel, with the output device. This stops the transistor being damaged by a back electromotive force (EMF) from the output device.

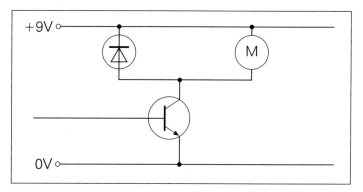

Relay

A **relay** is an electrical switch. It can be used to control another device that uses a different voltage from the electronic circuit. When the coil in the relay is energised by an electronic circuit, its contacts will change and switch the output device on.

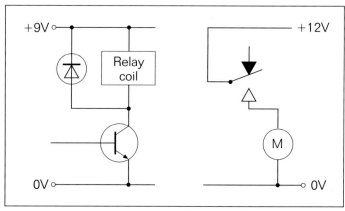

Solenoid

A **solenoid** works in a similar way to a relay. It converts electrical current into movement. A magnetic field is created when an electrical current is passed through a coil. This causes the soft iron core to move.

Solenoids can be used to lock doors and also to operate pneumatic valves. You can find out more about pneumatics on page 133.

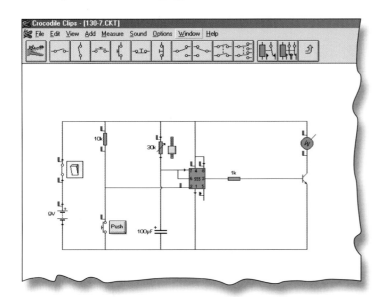

● **On task Develop your design**

1. On design sheet **7a**, draw a new system diagram to show how any additional features to your money box mechanism could be included.

2. Redraw your circuit diagram to include any additional features. You could simulate the operation of the circuit on a computer.

3. Modify the PCB design given to you by your teacher, to include any extra features. Show where each component will go. Do this on design sheet **7b**.

Remember

- The output current from an IC is very small.

- A transistor is used as a switch. This can be used with other output devices.

- A relay is an electrical switch that can be used to switch on output devices that use a different voltage from the electronic control circuit.

- A solenoid will convert an electrical current into movement and can be used to control a pneumatic system.

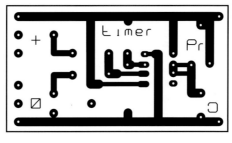

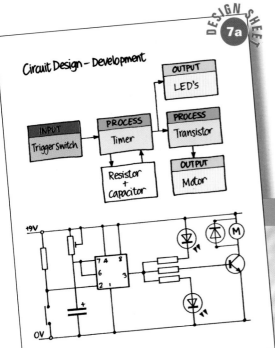

DESIGN SHEET 7a

Circuit Design – Development

● **On your design sheets**

- Draw a new system diagram. **7a**

- Draw your final circuit diagram. **7a**

- Show how you have modified the PCB design to include any additional features. **7b**

Making Models

Before you make a control system, you can model its operation using systems boards and a construction kit.

Pneumatics could provide another way of making your product come to life.

Modelling a large system

Before you make a **control system** that uses both electronic and mechanical parts you should **model** its operation.

In this way you can quickly check how well it works and make any modifications before you actually make it.

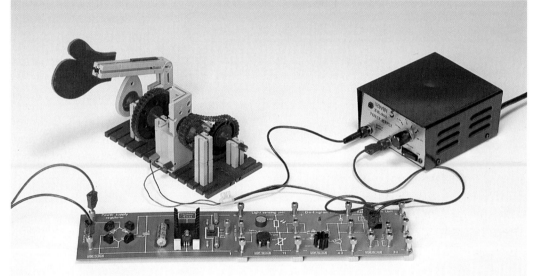

Fitting switch into money box

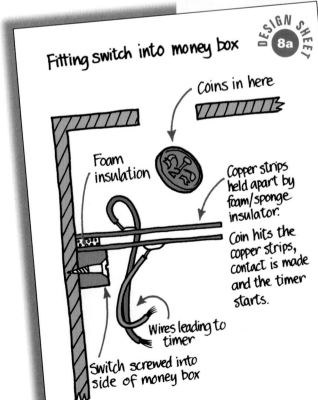

DESIGN SHEET **8a**

Coins in here

Foam insulation

Copper strips held apart by foam/sponge insulator.

Coin hits the copper strips, contact is made and the timer starts.

Wires leading to timer

Switch screwed into side of money box

Fitting the circuit

You will need to design and make a simple switch that will be struck by the money and then start the timer. It could be made from two thin pieces of copper. It is important to position the switch so the money will fall to one side, after striking it.

A small self-tapping screw can be used to hold your circuit to the base of the moneybox.

● **On task 1 Develop your design**

Design a simple switch for your money box. Show your ideas on design sheet **8a**.

Pneumatics

Pneumatic components and devices use compressed air to make the system operate. As with electronic systems they can be broken down into **input**, **process** and **output** components.

Pneumatics can be found in many aspects of our daily lives, such as tyres, pneumatic tools, and automatic door systems.

The air is compressed and stored in a receiver tank. A regulator controls the pressure of the air and its flow can then be controlled by use of valves. Using pneumatics is a safe and clean way of creating movement in a system.

Basic components

A 3 port valve is used to control the flow of air in a circuit. These valves are operated by a push button or by a solenoid. When the valve is depressed the piston rod of the single acting cylinder will move. When the valve is released, the piston will return because of a spring inside the cylinder.

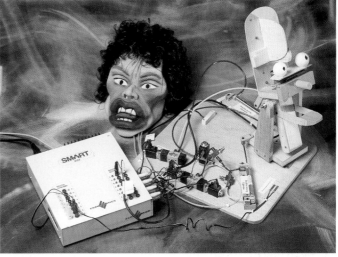

You could use a solenoid valve in an electronic system to control a pneumatic system.

● *On task 2 Develop your design*

On design sheet **8b**, redesign your system to include a pneumatic display. This could be used in a public location such as in a supermarket.

On your design sheets

- Record your ideas for a switch. **8a**
- Draw the system and circuit diagrams for your new design. **8b**

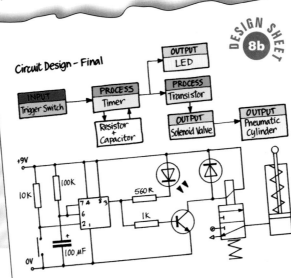

Remember

- Systems can be modelled, before they are made, to check they work.

- Pneumatics uses compressed air in a control system.

How Well Does It Work?

9

Before any product is put into use it needs to be tested to ensure it works reliably and safely. You will need to do this as part of your evaluation.

Making it work

Remember that to be successful, you will need to work carefully and accurately as you make your final product. Two particular things to pay attention to are soldering and checking the connections.

Soldering

▷ Are all the components in the correct place?

▷ Are all the components and PCB clean? Make sure you do not to touch the areas to be soldered.

▷ Have you allowed any small amounts of solder to melt between adjacent components? This could cause a short circuit.

▷ Don't forget to remove the soldering iron and trim any component legs.

▷ Did you remember to use a crocodile clip as a heat sink?

Checking the connections

It is important to check a circuit you've made carefully. If it does not work properly, check the following:

▷ Are the joints properly soldered?

▷ Are the components correctly connected?

▷ Are the components of the correct value?

▷ Are there any breaks in the PCB track?

You could use a **multimeter** to check the voltage at various points on the circuit.

Final evaluation

Once you have finished making your money box you will need to evaluate it. What changes or improvements could be made before it is used?

● On task 1 Final evaluation

Use the money box over a period of time at home to save all your spare change. Each time you use it consider the following points:

▶ Does the mechanism work smoothly, or does it jam or become tight at certain points?

▶ Does the money box work with all sizes of coin?

▶ Does the electronic circuit work reliably?

▶ Does the design continue to attract your attention? Has it encouraged other members of your family to use it?

Devise a specific test to evaluate a particular aspect of your money box in detail. Record what you discover on design sheet **9a**.

● On task 2 Final evaluation

Ask other people to use the money box. Ideally, this should include some younger children.

▶ What do they think of it?

▶ Do they feel the design reflects the charity you chose?

▶ Does it encourage them to give money?

▶ What suggestions for improvements can they make?

Complete the table on design sheet **9b** to record the responses of the people you ask.

● On task 3 Final evaluation

On design sheet **9c** explain:

▶ How any features of the money box that do not work reliably can be improved.

▶ How the mechanism and electronics could be re-designed to achieve a different effect?

Include your response to some of the suggestions made by others.

● On task 4 Develop your design

1. Suggest how your design could be modified to promote a different charity. Show your ideas on design sheet **9d**.

2. Design a different product that incorporates similar mechanical and electronic systems. For example, design a children's ride or a pedal waste bin. Describe how it could be made and how it would work. Use a construction kit to model your ideas. Use design sheet **9e**.

On your design sheets

● Record how well your money box worked over a period of time. **9a**

● Complete the table to show what other people said about your design. **9b**

● Suggest improvements to your design. **9c**

● Sketch ideas for other products that include mechanical and electronic devices. **9d/e**

Remember

● Rigorous testing will ensure your final product is reliable and safe to use.

An Interview with...

in the BOX

Trevor Baylis is the inventor of the clockwork radio. Here you can learn about how he thought up and developed his ideas.

BayGen

Where did you get the inspiration for the clockwork radio?

" Back in 1991 I was watching a programme about the spread of AIDS in Africa. The narrator was telling me about the need to get the health education message across to the population. A good way to do this was to use the radio, but in remote villages there is no electricity, and the cost of batteries can be as much as one month's income for just one set.

One of the things about being an inventor is that you always pick up on the word *need*. When somebody says there is a need for something, then generally speaking I get excited. "

What happened next?

" The first thing I did was to go to my little studio at the back of the house. I knew that an electric motor could be used in reverse as a generator. I found a very small motor which I then put into a hand brace. I was then able to hitch up two wires from that motor to the back of a very cheap transistor radio. And then from turning the handle I heard the first bark of sound from the radio – that was my Eureka! moment!

I suppose it took three or four months playing around with different types of springs and gears and so on, until it reached the point where I was able to put the radio together. It's a box which contains a fairly powerful spring. Then there's a gear box that the spring drives. In turn the gearbox drives a small generator which feeds electricity to a tiny radio. To make it work you simply wind the key.

After several more months development I applied for a patent. For £400 I protected my invention for a period of a year. This meant I had the sole rights to make and sell it. I wrote to Marconi, I wrote to Phillips, I wrote to British Petroleum, I wrote to National Power, I wrote to the Design Council. None of them showed any interest.

In April 1994 I got the opportunity to demonstrate my invention on the Tomorrow's World programme. Immediately after the programme I was absolutely deluged with phone calls from all sorts of lovely people who simply phoned up to say 'Well done!'

Amongst them was someone called Chris Staines. He was an acquisitions and mergers director of a company and had business contacts in South Africa. With his experience in product development he was able to start getting financial partners to put the radio into production. The Liberty Life Foundation became one of our backers on the basis that we would be setting up a multi-racial factory employing people of different abilities. **"**

Presenting Nelson Mandela with one of the first clockwork radios to come off the production line.

Months of testing and retesting, trial and error were vital to smooth out all the design modifications and ensure that when we went into production we would be making a radio that worked efficiently and was also pleasing to the eye. An industrial designer was brought in to sculpt the utilitarian box into a sleek, startling, streamlined shape.

In June 1995 I flew out to South Africa to see the factory. It was the most memorable day of my life. The workforce is totally integrated – black, white, brown, male, female, English, Afrikaans, Xhosa. The limbless work next to the blind, deaf people work in partnership with the able-bodied. **"**

How did the final product then take shape?

" There were still a lot of technical problems to solve. The spring I had first used was not powerful enough to produce enough volume for a long enough period. We did some market research and discovered that while there was a big demand for a clockwork-driven radio, Africans didn't want a miniaturised radio. They weren't much bothered about ease of handling, or how much it weighed; what they required was a radio that was big, heavy, very robust, and able to deliver a lot of noise.

What would you say was the key to your success?

" It's to risk thinking unconventional thoughts. Convention is the enemy of progress. If you go down just one corridor of thought you never get to see what's in the rooms leading off it. But having had your bright, fresh, original idea, the really hard part is turning it into a successful product. That's what takes all the sweat. **"**

● *On task   Have good ideas*

Where do you get your ideas from? Do you explore several alternatives, or just go down one corridor? Look back through your design work for this unit. Make notes on design sheet **10** about about how you developed your design ideas.

Product Design Dictionary

Aesthetics

Aesthetics is all about how people respond to things through their senses. What we see, hear, taste, touch and smell can be pleasant or distressing experiences.

Different people like and dislike different things. Generally, however, people respond well to things which are harmonious (i.e. go together well), or provide contrast (i.e. are opposites).

Which chair do you prefer?

Analysis

To analyse a product means studying it in smaller, more detailed parts. So, for example, if you were analysing a torch you would need to describe its casing, switch, battery, bulb, circuit etc.

Conflicting demands

Most design decisions involve making **compromises**. For example a rucksack needs to be strong but light. Products that are strong tend to use more material. Materials and components that provide a balance between strength and weight need to be used.

Meanwhile extra design features and materials that look good and last a long time are likely to increase the cost of a product. Other materials might be cheap and easy to work but cause environmental damage.

Components

Products are usually made up of a number of smaller parts, called components. Many components, such as transistors, screws, hinges, etc., are pre-made.

Consumers

Consumers are the people who will eventually use the products you are designing. Remember that consumers have a choice. If they don't want or like what you have designed, they won't use it. The particular group of consumers your product is aimed at is sometimes called the *target market*.

As you design, keep in mind exactly what people need physically and want emotionally. Your product needs to do the job the consumer wants it to, and make them feel good about using it.

Constraints

Constraints are things which limit the possibilities of your design. For example, there may be certain sizes, weights or types of materials you cannot use, or have been told you must use.

What sort of constraints might the designer of a new football have to consider?

Design brief, proposal and specification

The *design brief* is the starting point of a project or task. It usually contains general information about what is needed, who the product is intended for and any major constraints.

The design brief is usually provided by the *client*. This is the person who has asked you to design something for them. Your client could be from a large company, a local business, or simply someone you know.

Make sure you know who the users of your product will be. It will probably not be the client!

A *design specification* sets out in more detail what the final product needs to do. It states any minimum and maximum sizes, weights, safety requirements, costs, appearance, materials, methods of production, etc.

A *design proposal* is a suggestion for a possible solution that you present to someone else for their comments. Throughout a project you are likely to need to produce several design proposals for approval by your client (or in school your teacher) until you reach your final solution.

A *product specification* provides a precise description of the final product and how it should be made. It usually contains information about size, quantities, materials, components, methods of production, etc.

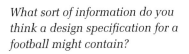

What sort of information do you think a design specification for a football might contain?

Environmental impact

Everything we make has an effect on the natural eco-system of our planet. There is a danger that the system could become permanently damaged. There is no such thing as a completely environmentally friendly product, but it is possible to reduce the impact and extent of the damage caused to help maintain a balance.

In your project work you should aim to produce designs that:

▷ use less materials and energy in their production

▷ can be re-cycled or reused and easily maintained.

Function

The function of a product means the things it is intended to do. A cup is made to hold liquids and look attractive. A watch needs to tell the time accurately and be small and light enough to wear on your wrist.

Many objects have more than one function. For example cups can also be used to measure ingredients. Others cups are used as trophies or as souvenirs.

As you design, remember that your product might have a variety of functions.

What other uses can you think of for a mug?

Information and communication technology (ICT)

Computers are changing our lives. They have also had a major impact on the way products are designed and made. There are many opportunities in D&T to use computers. Find out what facilities exist in your school. Think carefully about when it is appropriate to use them.

Computer-aided design (CAD)

There are many different types of CAD packages. Some are two-dimensional and are commonly known as drawing, paint or desk-top publishing or desk-top video programs. Others are three-dimensional, allowing the screen images to be turned and looked at from different angles. Some programs make animation in 2D or 3D easy.

Computer-aided manufacture (CAM)

Two-dimensional computer-aided designs can be printed out or saved to a disk. Data from three dimensional designs can be sent directly to machine tools which can produce solid objects automatically.

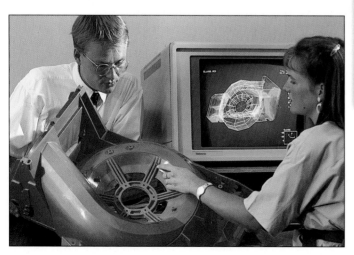

Control systems

Computers can be used to control sequences of events, turning circuits on and off, speeding things up or slowing them down and feeding back information from sensing devices to keep things running smoothly.

Databases

Databases are organised collections of information (text and/or images) which are held or organised on the computer. A database can be used to search, cross-reference and present information very quickly, and can be very useful during the investigating stages of a D&T project.

Destruction around the world

A storm surge is often more destructive than a hurricane's high winds. Surface water bulges beneath the storm's low pressure. Driven by the wind, the sea level rises, and battering waves crash inland. Whether by waves or by wind, hurricanes, also called cyclones or typhoons, can bring devastation. In 1970, more than half a million people died in a storm surge caused by a typhoon in Bangladesh. In 1991, Hurricanes Andrew and the flooding caused by it resulted in more than 30 billion dollars in damage in Florida—the costliest natural disaster in United States history.

Presentation packages

These programs enable you to present information on screen. You could use one to explain to an audience the main features of your design proposal. Words and images can be animated and sound and video sequences added.

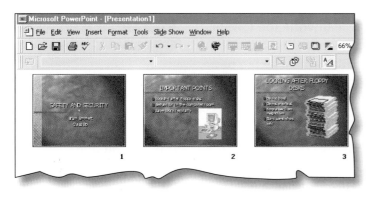

Spreadsheets

Spreadsheets help with complex calculations. Once set up they can be used to calculate the effect of changing one element of a design on all the other parts. The data from a spreadsheet can also be displayed quickly as a graph or chart.

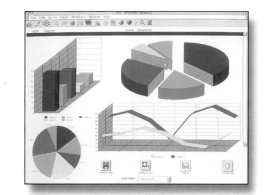

Word processing

Word processors are sophisticated typewriters which enable text to be checked and changed before being printed out. Word processed text can be easily placed into desk-top publishing programs where it can be laid out in columns and placed next to illustrations.

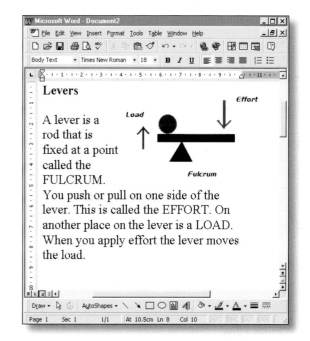

World Wide Web

The Internet (or World Wide Web) provides access to information from across the world. Search engines can help you find what you want.

You can also design web pages of your own. Many organisations have their own web sites.

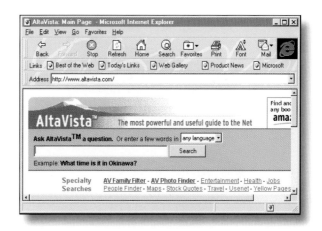

Manufacturing

There are a number of ways that products can be made:

▷ *One-off* production is where a single item is made on its own.

▷ *Batch* production is where a specific number of items are made together, saving time and materials. The production line can then be quickly changed to make a batch of a different design.

▷ *Mass* production is where identical products are made all the time. The different stages are usually carried out by different people, working on a conveyor-belt system.

Templates

These are useful in batch and mass production. They are standard shapes which can be used as a pattern for cutting identical pieces.

Jigs

Jigs are specially made tools which quickly place materials, tools and components in the right position.

Moulds

These are often used to produce identical copies of shapes and forms. Pliable or liquid material is usually placed over or in a mould. As it hardens it takes on the shape of the mould. Alternatives to moulds are *pressings* and *castings*.

As you develop your design ideas you will need to consider how they can be made as a one-off item in school and also in quantity.

Models and modelling

A *model* of a new design is often made to show a client or potential consumer before it is produced in quantity.

Meanwhile the idea of *modelling* is slightly different. Making new products takes a lot of time, effort and money, so it's a good idea to try your designs out as much as possible so that mistakes can be avoided.

To discover if something will work you don't necessarily have to make it the same size as the real thing, or use the same materials. Drawings, diagrams, mock-ups, prototypes, and test and trial pieces are all quicker and cheaper to create than the real thing.

In your D&T work think carefully about what you want to learn about your design from your modelling. Decide which is the best sort of model to make to get the information you need.

What sort of models might have been made of these sports products before they were mass-produced?

Presentation

The way you present your D&T work is very important. The sequence of sheets (or Design Folder) you hand in during or at the end of a project needs to show clearly the process you have used to investigate, develop, plan and evaluate your design ideas.

Remember that your design folder helps provide important evidence that you have achieved your targets. Good presentation won't cover up poor thinking, but evidence of good thinking can easily get lost if the presentation is poor.

Properties and characteristics of materials

Different materials behave in different ways. They are said to have different physical and chemical properties. For example a piece of plastic bends and melts when heated, while a piece of fabric burns. When some materials are processed or combined in a particular way their behaviour can change.

Sketches

Sketches are particular types of drawings used to record information and explore ideas. They should not be drawn very neatly using a ruler as this takes too long – they need to be quick so you can move on rapidly. Sketches often include notes or labels to help explain the ideas or to record passing thoughts. Sometimes they include colour, particularly if it is an important part of the design.

Workshop drawings

Unlike sketches, workshop drawings need to be very neat and accurate. They need to show exact sizes and shapes of all the materials and components needed to make the design. It should be possible for someone else to make up the design from your drawings.

Workshop drawings are usually laid out in *orthographic projection*, i.e. a plan and two elevations, with each part numbered and described in a table on the drawing.

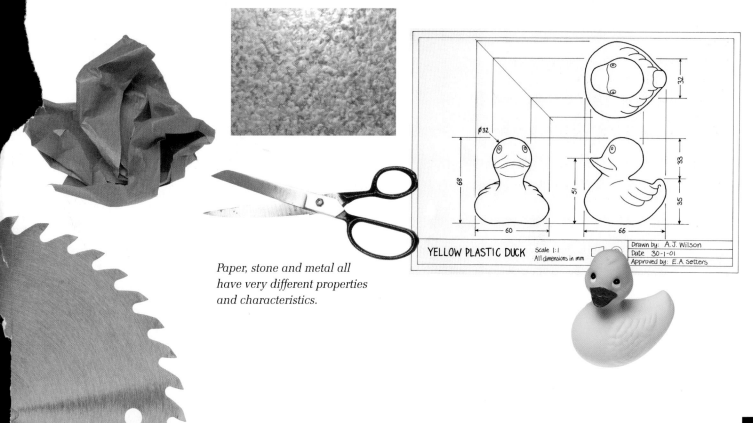

Paper, stone and metal all have very different properties and characteristics.

YELLOW PLASTIC DUCK   Scale 1:1   All dimensions in mm

Drawn by: A.J. Wilson
Date 30-1-01
Approved by: E.A. Setters

Index